Academy of Dreams

Academy of Dreams
New and Selected Poems

Glover Davis

LITERARY PRESS
LAMAR UNIVERSITY

ISBN: 978-1-942956-95-2
Library of Congress Control Number: 2022935859
Manufactured in the United States

Lamar University Literary Press
Beaumont, Texas

Acknowledgments

I appreciate the editors of the following publications in which some of the new poems first appeared.

Arts Alive San Antonio
Miramar
Poetry
Salt
San Antonio Review
Southwestern Review
Spillway
The Southern Review
Through Layered Limestone: A Texas Hill Country Anthology of Place

A long career inevitably incurs many debts. Mine has been enriched by teachers such as Phil Levine, Bob Mezey, and Donald Justice and by attentive and supportive poet readers like Christopher Buckley, Richard Katrovas, Peter Everwine, David St. John, Chuck Hanzlicek, and others. Former students have been enthusiastic supporters of my work, especially Marianne Werner, Gordon Preston, Rod Santos, Marian Haddad, David Martinez, Diana Garcia, Jane Milligan, Joe Milosch, and Michael Morey.

When I moved to Texas almost a decade ago, I was warmly welcomed into the poetry community of San Antonio by many writers: Roberto Bonazzi, Jim LaVilla Havelin, Naomi Shihab Nye, Palmer Hall, Octavio Quintanilla, Lahab Assef Al-Jundi, Natalia Trevino, Sheila Black, and so many others.

Jill Pugh was an invaluable assistant in the process of putting together this collection.

I'm grateful too for writer and editor Jerry Craven, who believed in my poetic vision enough to publish two of my books, including this one.

Recent Poetry from Lamar University Literary Press

Lisa Adams, *Xuai*
Bobby Aldridge, *An Affair of the Stilled Heart*
Michael Baldwin, *Lone Star Heart, Poems of a Life in Texas*
Charles Behlen, *Failing Heaven*
David Bowles, *Flower, Song, Dance: Aztec and Mayan Poetry*
Jerry Bradley, *Collapsing into Possibility*
Jerry Bradley, *Crownfeathers and Effigies*
Jerry Bradley and Ulf Kirchdorfer, editors, *The Great American Wise Ass Poetry Anthology*
Matthew Brennan, *One Life*
Mark Busby, *Through Our Times*
Julie Chappell, *Mad Habits of a Life*
Stan Crawford, *Resisting Gravity*
Chip Dameron, *Waiting for an Etcher*
Glover Davis, *My Cap of Darkness*
William Virgil Davis, *The Bones Poems*
Jeffrey DeLotto, *Voices Writ in Sand*
Chris Ellery, *Elder Tree*
Dede Fox, *On Wings of Silence*
Alan Gann, *That's Entertainment*
Larry Griffin, *Cedar Plums*
Michael Jennings, *Crossings, a Record of Travel*
Betsy Joseph, *Only So Many Autumns*
Lynn Hoggard, *First Light, Poems of Love and Loss*
Gretchen Johnson, *A Trip Through Downer, Minnesota*
Ulf Kirchdorfer, *Chewing Green Leaves*
Laozi, *Daodejing*, tr. By David Breeden, Steven Schroeder, and Wally Swist
Janet McCann, *The Crone at the Casino*
Laurence Musgrove, *Local Bird*
Benjamin Myers, *Black Sunday*
Godspower Oboido, *Wandering Feet on Pebbled Shores*
Dave Oliphant, *The Pilgrimage, Selected Poems: 1962-2012*
Kornelijus Platelis, *Solitary Architectures*
Carol Coffee Reposa, *Underground Musicians*
Jan Seale, *The Parkinson Poems*
Steven Schroeder, *the moon, not the finger, pointing*
Glen Sorestad *Hazards of Eden*
Vincent Spina, *The Sumptuous Hills of Gulfport*
W.K. Stratton, *Ranchero Ford/ Dying in Red Dirt Country*
Gary Swaim, *Quixotic Notions*
Waldman, Ken, *Sports Page*
Loretta Diane Walker, *Ode to My Mother's Voice*
Dan Williams, *Past Purgatory, a Distant Paradise*
Jonas Zdanys, *The Angled Road*
Jonas Zdanys, *Three White Horses*

For information on these and other Lamar University Literary Press books:
https://www.lamar.edu/literary-press/

To Mariana

CONTENTS

NEW POEMS

from
Bandaging Bread

Agnew's Abstract

Once before in a dream, I saw this place,
heard these same voices, saw these same faces.
I see the same patient, brush in hand, trace
long red circles across the slanted easel.
She carves the canvas with lines of pigment
with the uncertain, institutional yellow
of state buildings in massed blocks of cement.
I pause, the nurse with the tattooed arms,
the bleeding heart and the motto within
"God is Love," tells me, "For seven days and
seven nights, she has tried for the perfect,
the unbroken circle." But my old dream
returns, the details take on clarity.
The nurse hoops her head with the white-hot beam,
and Merlin in his Nazi helmet pulls
the gag, mutters spells and incantations.
My words float out to her but no one seems
to hear and the pack closes from all directions.
I break from this old dream frozen as before.

The Dreamer
For G.M.E.

Sitting, watching, hoping for something new
he put his cup against the light as if
it were a negative. He saw the blue

white china cup within his hand begin
to pulse, the rim expand and whiten at
the mouth, until the bridge, the stunted pine

and the twisted cypress stretched before him
like a dream. He heard the tinkle of the wind
in the glass trees and tore pebbles from the limb.

He came to the great pagoda with its blue tower
and climbed to where the sky meets the designs.
He saw above his head the pale flower

and tore some petals loose and ate, looking
for doors or windows where there were only
the painted panels and more roofs. Locking

his fingers in the quilted leaves he climbed
up past the timberline to the icy slopes
and saw, below, the coffee stream like lead.

He dropped a pebble in the pool and felt
the circles like the targets of his eyes
expand to the cupped white skin and melt.

The Fish Tank

I sit watching TV and a parade
of pills, bottles, soaps and blades punishes
but gives me dreams. Sometimes the dreams invade

my waking hours and I live on the edge of things
where the curtains puff with meaning, the chairs
hold themselves with dignity and the wings

of the ebony table are resilient
with a power which they won't use. The things
I see are tense, disciplined and sapient.

I scoop up pebbles from the goldfish tank.
I touch them for their hardness. One is clouded
and glazed like a dead eyeball that's gone blank

with nothing to see. I see the fish caught there
in the water, their veins shot with stone, the
barbeled mouths turned up pulsing at the air.

Bandaging Bread

Police will cluster
along the borders of the ghettos.
The precincts will pulse like wounded flies.
People are burning, L says,
everything rocks in a film of heat.
He lifts two loaves of black bread
from the map on his kitchen table.
This bread is taped like dynamite
for the C.I.A. is everywhere
and we must practice.
The time is coming,
we cannot hold it back,
when the wounds of the table
will swell like blossoms.
The time is coming, he says
pointing to a bridge,
a loaf here,
and the bridge will rise like dust,
the suburbs will settle and fill with light.

From the Dark Room

People buy sunglasses, beer, oil their skins
and change their clothes like elms putting up shields
of green, but still the heat presses. I wince
as every sonic boom shakes trays and winds

seem to sweep out of the dark; the red that glows
from the ceiling light dances across the waves
until my rubbered hand stops everything.
I see the world in pictures. When light flows

through delicate patterns of leaves or clouds
they stiffen and wait for the thunder. But the film
is there like raw tissue open to the light.
I see in photos, people strung in crowds

on the beaches, in the streets, on the pavements
black with heat where people run and are caught
by bursts of flashbulbs, or where alone and guilty
they turn on their lives in these explosive moments.

They seem the same unlike the bulbs that heat
has left clouded and split with veins. But I
am here alone as always, feeling fine.
I turn from my work a few times a day to eat.

I noticed yesterday the negative
of school children caught at play, their features
like charcoal, their hair, lips and eyes a luminous
expanding white, the sky black and tentative.

The Pilot

Takes my hand
and the syllables slip
from his burned mouth

like compressed air.
Dazed by whiskey
he speaks of water

of the gray
fields of the sea
which mean safety

and of the villages
he never sees, rocked
in a dream of fire.

His hands balance
like wings showing
me that angle

where bodies lighten
and eyes stream with fire.
When I close my eyes

I see dust spurt
from his goggles
or dance like flame

along the clear
panels of plexiglass.
"Touch me," he says,

"touch me when I sleep
or when I dream."
When I touched him

he was five. I am his mother
and I paint the bad knee
that bled and bled.

Monuments

The lines on your stone tablets are the lines
that slowly carve themselves into my face.
I see your chiseled cups, flowers and lace,
the grass being cut, the gophers building mines,
and legions of crows circling to attack the pines.
A dead man settles in a dark blue vase;
the shifting of his ashes has the grace
of shifting dust. The weeds push back the vines.
I feel as if I also were becoming
a monument with a few sad lines the winds
have cut in stone. All my life with all my death
I will remember these words. The growing
of the grass will push through pores that nothing binds
and I will eat my grayness with the earth.

from
August Fires

The Burial

The birds have stripped
the fig tree.
The fruit is ripped
and the bees
are hovering near
the loose skin.
I try to scare
birds with tin
can lids I string
like flashing
necklaces. A wing
beats a leaf
blue and the jays
erupt
through the leaf maze
but high up
where crown leaves
   take
the sun, hawk
in a lake
of light green sways.
Mockingbird
dives and red
from the blurred
feathers spreads
where the hawk climbs.
I remember
a curved beak
a black ember
for an eye
how the mate
would circle and cry
as I fit
the other
in a box.
When a shut
lid knocks
beneath my thumbs
and the dirt

rains down and numbs
my mind
I awake to find
my heart pumps
like a wing without air.

The Orphan

I saw her near Anaheim by the fence
in a black fur coat from the trash.
The wind ruffled her blond hair, tugged
at the black fur. She pointed with an oily wrench,
a streaked scepter, and her lips
murmured a song. I was five miles
down the freeway before I turned the car
and found among the packing cases, glass,
stripped fenders nothing but a piece of silk
and a crayon drawing on slate, a girl
with a glowing crown and a house
near a green river beyond acres of cars.
I remember the cheekbones tipped with rouge,
the tears blurred, and then the long ride
back to the orphanage, the cold sandwich
and the beating in front of everyone.
The locked room where she must kneel
under a thick belt and a sister's habit
unfurling like a pirate flag would rise
in a book full of crosses. Bells sound
in the stone courtyard where the children march
in robes and slippers, and the traffic stalls
forever in the calm lanes of the wind.

Dreaming Bear

in my worst dream someone I cannot see
bends down and whispers lies into my ear.
I feel the furred hand sliding through my hair.
I hear one grunt and watch him rise like a tree.
dirt from his ankles spreads dark roots. I free
one leg from the swirled sheet and branches tear
like tissue from the ribs of a struck deer.
the bears buzz softly over me.
a bee bumps glass and everything goes still.
dark, gentle ones who sway and burn through brain
or blood, when I awake, your moon-stained fur
is gone and the red tongues that searched my will
are damp spots on the pillowcase. Your pain
blows out of my fierce eyes and will not blur.

Dreaming Bear II

the bear is a dark wound, and when I dream
of bears, I always see thick fur and blood.
I sleep in strange forests where whispers flood
the air. white fluttering of a headlight's beam
and then cold air and light that blurs with steam
these sad, new eyes. my hair wilts like a bud
in this clear stream that picks up flaws; fresh mud
on my red coat, hurt faces in the stream
of their own breathing dark. I am like Cain.
my neck fur riffles in a sudden breeze
the trailing leaves, vines, birds, all things that stick
and burn I dream; the bear's red seal of pain
is a curved mouth, a heart that will not freeze
a steaming wound I delicately break.

The Eagle

late march. rain for weeks. when it stops I'll walk
through the arroyo and listen for the fox
in the mint loose and wild a red-tailed hawk
a poppy's petals white and drooped like cloth.
but even as I peel an onion   I find
smog in the wings and the pearled heart streaked.

animals of earth and water, the snake
the gopher and the frog are holding on.
even the smaller birds thrive when the heat
thickens the air and eagles flutter down.
the olives grain with soot. because I take
this message from the onion with all its tears

I pour water on a leaf and watch the edge
steam and curl, the brown veins drink.
I saw two eagles at the city dump
thrown away   wings smoking like newspaper.

The Clouds

VI
black angel in the graveyard
at Iowa City   the bronze wings
above the tablets
of snow.   the lindens steam.
whirlwinds of paper
and soot soiling the snow.
the woman is buried beneath
saplings shining in the ice
no memory of the husband
who disappeared   the Polack
    bar
where she would make it
with anyone.   one night
we crossed markers   name
    plates
marble crosses and saw
the statue trembling in
    wind
feet shod with damp black
    leaves
green rust from the eyes
and mouth   the bronze features
of the face bitten
by the inexpressible cold
that must have gripped her
    mind.

Helios

In the mountains east of San Diego
the high grass whispers.
After a month of rain, the fields
are shocked with mustard and wild lilacs.
Acorns caught in the crevices of burnt oaks
bloom from the dead branches
and summer, hazed, sweet, white
summer comes again.

II
In the rush of things
from the center, sap and honey, ground water
steeped in granite, wax pods split,
tongues leak pure air.
Upturned bees in a cloud
of crimson half an inch
above the fan-shaped petals.

III
The green jade mountain rides
the storm of color,
fire trails touch off lungs, heart
the rippling trail of blood
blossoming under my skin, sobs,
swells of muscle,
undulations pouring inward on the startled eye
unshaken by dynamite, sourced like a mountain.

IV
Holocaust of mouths: pointed
tongues of plants
drift from burning odors of leaves.
By noon the flank of the mountain
is swaying, nature's poor,
driven by the wind
toward pools of asphalt on the road below.

V

Bulldozer, tract house, dynamite
5 yrs. away and the imagination flutters
a burnt rag of surrender above the city.
Dusk and the light comes in
over slopes, boulders. Shadows pool
the purples and the greens. Below us
white flocks of pigeons dot
rising blooms in a meadow of air.

VI

The mad, red hair of the poppy
floats toward the sun. Its stem, an anchoring
torso. It tugs like a blimp.
Ten of them in my hand; the red pulse grains
my arm. My head is magnetic for blood.
I pray to the roots of the oak.
Helios in the blood
in the last drunken daze of sun.

Leather Jacket

I put my jacket on a boulder
and went back down the path.
picked   straw daisies   tied blue
washed rocks   in a hanky.
when I returned   my jacket
was full of air.   the black creases
of the elbow   were sailing
down the cliff.   skull
and crossbones painted
on someone else's back.
when I looked inside
I saw   white stretch marks
a few clumsy stitches.   the neck
gradually darkened with sweat
and became smooth.
from the first day
I wore it like armor.
neat's-foot oil rubbed in
deckles of light.
I was a deer   or a lion
a leopard in his fiery spots
heart   beneath the cross hairs
opening   like a shot wineskin.
when the seams pull apart
I open all at once
words pouring through my fingers
every part of me   a target.
I move quickly to the
edge of the cliff and watch
my jacket dangle   far below
from a bush   as if the bush
were a man with habits.
I could imagine the sudden step
into air and the mind
crying no !   I could almost see
the white blades of the shoulders
driven through skin.
I climb down these rocks
like a man rescuing a friend.

The Midway

I swam from a cargo net
somewhere near the Philippines.
5 feet under   the water
so blue   so clear   it
was air.   back on the
carrier I could smell
diesel everywhere.
H bombs draped with cloth
came out of the pit
below the mess deck.
we were bored. we ignored
bombs   marines with
special clearance in
dress blues   and concentrated
on our steaks.
                    we could've
burned down any city
burned the air
or the water   turned
half of China into a river
of stone.
            I tended
a Doppler radar that
        whistled
like a bird and charted
landing speeds.   once
we gathered above the
flight deck   the wind
fluttering our jumpers
and watched a jet crash land.
sparks foamed up the
fuselage. a piece of wing
hit a bulkhead
and that was all.

First Class Petty Officer

Evans used to bawl us out
almost every day. once
when the laundry came
back and there was oil
on the deck
we smeared his clean clothes
put it on his pillow
a little puddle in the
middle of his blanket.
all of us swore it was
some engineers we'd never
seen before.
                Evans said
he wanted another war
wanted us all in so he
could shave our heads
and it was coming and he
would be in charge of all
the mama's boys   they'd
have to get tattooed.
and he'd make sure
that we ate it.
he'd be there in a bar
in Hong Kong with a bottle
of San Miguel. he'd watch
the woman throw away
her gardenia   bend back
across a wet table   all the
sailors whistling   and
stamping   all the kids
going down for the first
    time.

Liberty

A 12 year-old girl
danced with the
sailors. stiff and frightened
she kept looking
back for the fat one
who smiled and waved her on.
she had a red
camellia in her hair
and too much rouge
as if she'd gotten
into mother's make-up.

I bought monkey meat
on a stick, bottles
of San Miguel and watched.
my stomach flared.
my head went down
and there were women
asking me for drinks.
I gave them bills
colored like the rainbow
and left.
        anchored
in the harbor
the hulks washed
in moonlight,
the metal softened.
I took a jitney
back to the pier
refused cockfights,
whores, anything I wanted
and swayed up the
ladder in a long line
of sailors. some moaned
or dreamed.
I carried a drunk
bosun over my shoulder
one of his shoes
was gone   his wallet lost.

an officer, pretending
not to notice, gave back
our liberty cards.

who knew there'd
be burning issues
and the v.d. line
would coil around
the hangar deck?

Tattoos

after our first
liberty half of the
sailors came back with
tattoos. I had never
seen such a use
of skin. a heart
hopped when a muscle
flexed   a tiger bled
a forearm   and then
the scabs puffed like
cotton. everyone
was sorry. I almost
had a scarab inscribed
on the web of my thumb
in honor of my uncle
who had one there.
I could see my hand
red or blue
like a lip   and thought
of the gold stuck
on the collars of officers.
we'd wear animals
forever. we'd be
like pets.
          my skin
breathes   tans
lightly or fades
mottled by leaves or
water marks when light
bounces from waves.
I knew the day was
coming when I'd strip
jumper,   white hat,
bell bottoms, bundle
them into an incinerator.
no birds on my arms
reminding me of the
ensign smelling undershirts
for sweat   the smudge

on shoes polished
like mirrors where
his face comes back
from my foot.

Sanctuary

first Sunday at the convent and a nun
dresses me in a business suit. she makes
me shine my shoes, comb my hair and run
to the entrance hall with my brother and sister
to wait for my mother's visit. The month before

in a brown paper sack, she packed a loaf
of bread, jars of peanut butter and jam
and when my sister dropped the jam, she cried
and tried to pick the glass from strawberries—
no more money and we would have to march

like soldiers down the paths into the trees
and listen to the animals, the crow
who warned her or the squirrel, rabbit, fox.
the flashing of bright wings could mean the end.
St. Michael spoke to her and the gentle wind.

I remember the day: the sun was hot,
my starched collar damp with sweat.
I was 12—first soft hairs of beard on my cheek.
and then the yellow cab was there. I saw
her in the back seat, skin pulled tight around

her face   bones of the skull showing through.
her voice from a distance   from somewhere else
"no food in days   slept all night in the park."
the three of us wept on the sidewalk
until a nun came in her warm, black cape

and took us back   back to the chapel where
the candles flickered and there was incense
and light that poured from the stained glass,
and on my knees I dreamed my first real dreams
of peace. the steaming light that touched us there

a dim red on the foreheads of the others
who knelt beside me   all of us hurt, and one
of us without fathers.   Now I

visit her in a cinder block motel
where she washes sheets and towels, scrubs the floors.

the owner, Fred, who kept her, fed her, loved
her 14 years is dead. drunk or sad
she phones and says nothing over and over.
I try to quiet her and not get mad.
her mind circles and circles and won't let go

it's finally time and when I stand she looks
at me with my own eyes. the motel light
is blinking on her wall—her lips, her brow,
my face as it will be in a few years.
she smiles and says "this pain is all I have."

August Fires

Drove all day from San Diego
up the great trail of ashes
in my rearview mirror the eyes
of truck drivers benzedrined
a broken truck outside of Newhall
thousands of oranges spilled
a woman crying   I didn't stop.
Signs everywhere in the mountains
radar towers   smoke lookouts   mirrors flashing
200 miles to go   I keep pushing
and think "a singing bird will bring
the message"   drops of oil fall
from his wings   down from Santa Barbara
where the beach gasps through its coating.
Firebird over Topanga
a shower of sparks two miles high
hot winds blowing in from the deserts
the mountains purifying themselves
and no one learns.

II
There's a red dot in a scrawl
of lines on the road map.
I touch the places where my friends live
hundreds of miles away.
I was lonely once and talked
to no one. I sat in the shade next
to my trailer through the afternoons
watching a squirrel or a hawk
and did not read or write.
The sand burned my feet and the
dry stalks whispered. I killed
a rattlesnake that summer
and the white hiss struck through the air.
Part of him was smooth
and the red lines crossed like diamonds.
I thought of how he mapped the ground
with his belly. Grit in the flaps
and the thick coils looped over

a stick. I oiled the rifle
showered   and drove 500 miles.
Now I drive to the spot
where the red lines join like a heart.

III
Fog swirls down Golden State   fenders turning
into flares   the truck horns blaring past
Delano coming up   snow crust above
Grapevine   my breath clear as frost
at this altitude she smiled and touched
my forehead to see if I was tired
patches of ice beside the road
a smeared pine against the ridge   cold blue
and metal everywhere.
                              L.A. far below us
in a blanket of fumes   neon lights
like a glowing wind rushing toward
the sea   we paused in the clear streams
of air and watched the water
burning down the stone ducts of mountains.

IV
someone is grinding the faces
of the poor. their sweat rags smoking
their brows charred   a deputy
shows them the long way down into
the valley flowing with metal.
a little black dog smudges the air.
a man gnarled and tougher than a tree.
words break loose like the branches
of his life. the prayers of the poor go up
like smoke from the ghettos 30 miles south.

Eddie brought me here one morning   praising
with the eye of the painter   sweeping
his arms along the valley like brush strokes
the deep greens   the blond shadows sweeping in
from Malibu   this is for all of us
he said   I remember the swift hand
of his imagination striking
out fence posts   boundaries   the inked

41

poisons of real estate coming down
now in a rain of smoking paper.

V
Leaflets of fire along the highway
near Ft. Tejon race toward the trees.
the dial on my speedometer flutters
like a pine needle.   I watch   fire sparrows
stones melting   oak trees blessing
the flames and far below   a tract
of houses flares into dust
mesquite crackles toward the grove
and the wind turns.
smoke in my skin and hair
I pick the ashes from my collar.
I kneel in a ruined meadow
and find in a handful of earth
the three shining seeds of the poplar.
tail lights at dusk
like candles to the sun.
the cars keep coming   and coming.

VI
Allan holds the book of changes
and the words change into ideograms
black lines   on snow white rags   steaming branches.
He says man is like a tree in the pale earth.
He holds a saucer up to the light
and points to the opaque moons
two pale wings in glass.
Behind us the hills are boiling
and the almond barely stirs.

We drink our tea.   He says   the Chinese
would have cherished these August Fires.
His eyes are like the eyes
of the sage on my tea cup   glowing eyes
that miss nothing   the radiant mass
of the mountains.   the pines exploding
20 miles away. He goes on praising
a petal from an almond tree.

VII

50 houses   puffed
like parchment   used cars
melted into grease   dogs
with a mottled thighbone
pipes   chimneys   twisted iron
of bedsteads   wind humming
through a black refrigerator.
I touch the chalky feathers
of the pine   and reach for
the cypress cup where I drank
my own breath.   Blue fog
from my lungs beads the lips
of the men hand-loading   canvas hose
pickaxe   shovels and gunny sacks.
Rabbits streak from the red valleys.
And the rain behind my heart
full of swords months away
from the purple heart-shaped
fruit of the cactus.

VIII

There's a stained lunch sack
and a cup of coffee
in which a petal floats
but the workers sleep
in the shade until
a burning thistle drops
like a sword through their dreams.
They brush the grass
from their shirts and
take the path flung
through the heat like
a branch deflected on
the water.   I watched
and dozed and read my book.
I did not see the veins
of an oak leaf in the
hide of a deer or the
butterfly who turned
white hot in a second.

IX
Let the manzanita go
like a prayer wheel tipped
with rockets   a burning rag
of the seagull flutter down.
Let the butane spread
through the stained air
of California   the oil slick
billow like a robe of gold
from the harbors   let the
barbed wire leap from its post
the eagle and the fox return
like pieces of light.

from
Legend

Barometer

I rise at 6 a.m. clearing a space
among my papers for a glass, a plate
and drink my black coffee while I erase
some lines, thinking again of those I hate
or fear—their images annihilate
in the construction of this poem—and know
as I accumulate details that flow

from memory and try to trace their roots
that what I hated most was sometimes part
of me, but a screen of eucalyptus mutes
a flaring horn and streams of metal start
to move as I eat, wishing this poem could chart
the impulse irresistible as pain
that floods my mind and when it ebbs, its stain

is there like yellow sweat into a shirt.
I put away the breakfast things and wash
and concentrate again on those I've hurt,
on those who've injured me but when the lash
of tongues, gossip that wounds or turns to ash
whatever its mind touches, fixes me
I am like needles stuck as a bright sea

darkens, but even now when it is calm
and I am balanced, clear and lean above
my kitchen table, head propped on my palm,
I find I am unable to forgive.
I had hoped that through these lines I could live
without distortion that even the dark
rising through my unconscious like the mark

of Cain would clear and that this act would blot
from memory the guilt that wrecks my time.
This is not penance; this cannot unclot
the bloodless tangle of invented crime
which I project, watching my brothers climb
like wounded swimmers waters of a dream
where their breaths run into a whirling stream.

Illegal Alien/ El Salvador

A campfire fumes below us in the dark.
We know that he is back, his bedroll spread
on sand beneath a tent of brush and bark.
He sleeps and shivers not from cold but dread.
Last year he ran below a chopper's blades
its winds so strong it beat the bushes flat.
But this is not the source of what pervades
all waking moments but images of bloated
corpses where flies have darkened tender skin.
He does not dream the four American nuns
but the blood-soaked eyes of a young cousin,
holes punched in her smooth brow where men let guns
rest as she knelt in mud in a blue dress.
Because almost a child yet, she could hope
that nothing much would happen; she could press
her hands as though she feigned fear and the rope
around her neck would loosen when mama
called through the dusk these boys in uniform
"Eugenio, Roberto, suppertime, papa
will scold you if you're late," but the tape worm
fear living in eyes, eats till they can't see
their sister; till they can squeeze gleaming half moons
of metal, young lords with signet rings who free
from a wet eye all puzzling, light tangling runes.
If caught and cuffed I know he'll wait somewhere
below familiar lights that burn above
the hills of Tijuana—planets drenched in air.
One moonless night he'll cross again and move
up the arroyos like an animal.
I think of him when a cat's eyes glow green
at night in brush like candles in a skull.

From Poland to the Orphanage 1948

His pin striped suit was patched where
the breast pocket had been ripped
away—clipped head almost bare.
At lunch time his quick eyes slipped
from our forks to his own plate.
He held a package with one
hand and watched us as he ate.
In his eyes no expression
no tremor in a brown hand
locked to a fork but later
in the yard when we poured sand
in his hair, muddy water
in his cuffs, he only laughed.
When he frowned there was a crease
darkening his brow like a draught
in stone, his nine-year-old face
marked like a man's as he tried
to speak to us in Polish.
Though the other new kid cried
that first night, dampening with fresh
tears his pillowcase, Paul slept
and moved next morning down long
aisles where most of us had wept
beneath our blankets, a song
on his lips, towel, toothbrush,
soap in his hands and no fear
of the bullies who would push
him out of line and then sneer
at his words, his thick cheekbones.
They were to him only walls
bumped in the dark, or the stones
one must shake from socks, or scrolls
of breath and soap he whispered
onto the mirror, then wiped
with a sleeve. But he left spurred
crystals melting there, the piped
steam rising, no memory
of crystals dropped in acid
his mother's face in a sea

of gas, white and washed with dread.
Paul was passed from farm to farm
until the war was over
and then a camp where the harm
done children was a river
of pages cased in metal.
Days later a foreign priest
would translate those wild words Paul
painted on the air, a feast
of syllables none of us
would taste until the priest spoke.
We wanted then to discuss
his life but when a tear broke
from an eye we were silent.
His eye of stone and water
glowing like a new planet
his voice with its slight flutter
made us see, for the first time,
the boy beneath features carved
from rock—like birth the long climb
out, the trembling lips pain carved.

Your Father's Hands
for Larry Levis

I remember the uncoiling threads of smoke
from a gun's mouth weaving the dust in light
as a struck pigeon plopped into the barn's
dirt, a whirlpool of feathers at your feet,
and the quick beak of a blade flashing light
as it arced toward a throat until your father
caught the wrist and broke it on a tractor's treads.
But after the reading when I introduced my son
you had to excuse yourself for a minute,
step into the patio before the tears
went coursing down the causeway of your cheeks.
I learned as much about you in those minutes
as I had learned from years of casual friendship.
You missed your son who visits twice a year
and skis with you on the slopes miles above
Salt Lake on tiny skis that plow the white
powders you wipe from his eye brows, his cheeks—
his features just like yours when you were five.
When you were five your father's hands would comb
and button, hands that flamed in the vineyards
when heat rained down. One gentle hand would rest
like Isaac's blessing on your tousled head
the other perched a second on your shoulder
the way a falcon would before it rose
taking your mind with it into the blue
into such height and depth the place you stood,
the black pool of your shadow was a speck.
Night after night one dreaming hand has flapped
within a darkened copse of sheets and quilts
where you have seen the issuing of the crows
at dusk, their hundred darting wings above
the other hand that will not beat, that curls
like a fetus on your thigh till both are still
and no symbolic wings will raise your son.

Lost Connection

I'm on my way in the back seat of a car.
Ashes spill through the tops of cracked windows
and glowing motes extinguish on the air.
Above, the sky is blue but checked by crows,
a thousand slanting wings inked on a page.
The driver's hands are shaking on the wheel.
He smiles and points ahead to a mirage.
He whispers harshly "this is so unreal.
You have awoken from another dream.
This is a trip you took once as a child."
All of his words are wreathed in plumes of steam.
"If one should die, by choice unreconciled
to what he truly is, he would be caught
beyond time's limitations in a place
where seat belt buckles and the doors are hot,
where all the levers freeze and every face
that fills a rearview mirror is so strange
he will slide fingers over eyes and lips."

I dial the telephone but the exchange
is dead only the driver's cool voice slips
like wind through the worm holes of the black cup.
A pane of darkened glass begins to rise.
A sea gull or a burning rag goes up.
I shout and rap the glass but the driver sighs
looking ahead, adjusting his black robe.
There's static till, for moments at a time,
the dead receiver clears and voices probe
the clashing frequencies, describing crime
in progress, disasters natural and unkind.
Modulation may still sine waves that run
wild, with a voice from the electronic wind:
who in the world are you and what have you done?

The Apparition

They find him sleeping on the ground
as early heat begins to burn
the grove and wake him gently, turn
him toward blurred faces and the sound

of traffic. He tries to tell them why
he drinks and how he came to be
here desolate in the debris
of cans and bottles but they sigh

and measure skid marks, write his name
on their tablets as the chrome bars
fall from the grill like teeth or stars
of glass. The shields on their breasts flame.

One puts a bandage on his brow
(the others mottle under leaves)
but if he thinks the hot light weaves
a semblance of wings pale as snow

along their arms and shoulder blades
he's seeing only what he wants
and the mythology that haunts
his reverie with light now fades.

Care

After a day of reigning heat I tend
a drooped crookneck, making the leaves that shrink
all day now slowly stiffen as streams link
the furrows, cooling the stalk and the root end.
But at noon squash buds streak orange and I bend
to touch a mouth split as though it might drink
the light, as though now its furred tongue might sink
into a cup where bees tumble and pend.
And wonder why I care about these plants
dreaming and spreading through the August heat.
It must be pungent drifting leaves that glance
my brow or the slight cling and curl, discreet
as a girl's touch, but I weed, break the trance
I envy, cut the fruit I'll never eat.

Running with the Elephants

Everyone else is faster
lighter. Our bulk
our bibs of sweat
make us seem
like different animals.
Gudgel kneels
on the grass
his helmet still on
and spews. Rod
sings to himself
snapping his fingers
his beer belly
foaming over
his buckle.
My heavy pads
bounce, my heels blister
in the new cleats.
I need water, shade
I need to rest
beneath the tree
where the backs
who lapped us
sit unlacing shoes.
No one laughs at us
imitates the way
we run because
tomorrow we'd knock
the air from them
make them gasp
like punctured tires.
I love the way
my body takes
the shock, the way
my thick legs drive
when I catch
a back on my shoulder
and root him out.
Later in the locker room
we look into mirrors

without armor
smearing our combs
with pomade.
We're pale, twenty pounds lighter,
sixteen years old.
In a few minutes
we'll step from the gym
into the sunlight
blinking, heads down
our huge trunks
swaying as we walk.

Winter King

Sometimes ships ice in a harbor so dark
the little lights extinguish one by one
and blue fields the mind cuts—contrails and wakes
even the passionate glitter of snails—
expunge as though a damp eraser sighed
sweeping above, then to the angel pray
for dispensation from Lethe's blessing,
and for thoughts more stately in passage than
   swans
that pulling slowly from the past candesce
as though dreadnoughts crossed the T on each one.
If there is such a thing as a spring thaw
at my age—spars and rigging melting free—
then I will move once more through the ether.
This heavy body not so much a hull
as cloth drinking the wind or lunar tides
in blood or brain tugging me toward a blue
so vast I long for the casements of ice.

Beneath Venetian Blinds

When the angel spoke through lattices of flame
you napped, lethargic in the summer heat
and what those fluttering bands of light might claim
from you, you would not see as beat by beat
wings hammered into blue and disappeared.
You thought it was only the wind in blinds.
You thought the panes where two worlds might have sheared
light stippled, moist—where imagination assigns
to pure intelligence an aureole
of blood or whatever else the heart may need
could be ignored and it was easy, dull
and torpid as you were till bead by bead
the drumming sprinkler made the colors run.
A darkening room impelled you toward the glass.
Your cheek a hot house petal, pressed and dun,
stuck with your breath and hair in a morass
of bluish green, a knuckle might have smashed.
Beyond all this there was a garden laved
with air and trellises where the wind slashed
branches swept up a light, red buds engraved.
But you had missed the import when you ignored
gardens for syllables that spelt distress.
Thinking that this is what the flaming sword
of Eden is, you rose at dusk and dressed.

Even Our Statues Dream for Us

Our chairs sink in dirt, light splotches our hands.
White roses are trembling against our knees.
If we murmur our pens are like black wands.
If we rise, legs are as feathers the winds seize.
Therefore, we nap or watch the petals drop
hoping a bell will toll and thrushes cloud
the branches, disturbing air or blossoms with prop-
wash of their wings and once again we'll crowd
a page with textures of a leaf or wing.
But now the tulips fenced with lath and string
shiver and burn as water touches them,
the fountain's pattern broken by the wind.
It seems as though this stone is flesh, this hem
tapping a brittle ankle seems designed
to border rigid cloth just as it shreds
in chiseled lines—we think of Merlin immured
forever in a rock off Cornwall as foam spreads
around his knees and of a bright, wrenched sword
sunk in a lake—all through the long noon hour
we fitfully doze in open capes of stone
until through turning leaf blades a pale shower
might flood stiff hands and soften them to bone.

Lost Moments

There is a darkness, dark
as a tunnel where a boat
rocks and its oarlocks creak
as chills settle in your throat.
If you can see the faint
pulse of a cigarette
or hear the murmuring plaint
of voices, you might regret
lost moments in a shaft
of light that set the roses
trembling. Perhaps you laughed
at what the light imposes
on petals or your skin.
You smoked watching the pond
glaze gold and then went in.
Though dreams or darkness spawned
this place, it is no different
from the garden if you think
of your end, and of a current
through time you cannot blink
away as though it were
a lightless dream. It drifts
its deckled light through a pure
air. It leads and lifts
unless you think that this
tunnel of love is all
there is, then waters hiss
beneath the blades and oil
glistens on the crushed cups
and papers floating by.

The Wedding Feast

At the wedding feast tables loaded with loaves
bottles of wine and flowers in massed banks
stood in meadows where blossoms fell from groves
of orange and pear, cloth dressing the rough planks.
I knew that soon the others would be here.
But there's a stillness as I bend to pick
daisies, lilacs. Petals prick thumbs and fear
comes flooding in until an eyelid's quick
shudder unfocuses and the dreamed place
dissolves again in sleep and yet I wish
for the unremembered scene which I erase
on waking, slowly rise, look with a fresh
eye at an urban world, its streaming cars
on the freeway below my house and feel
a discrepancy in time and place which mars
the passing moments, knowing what I seal
in sleep is always there. But when I think
of stone jars full of water turned to wine
there is a silver brook from which I'd drink,
a chalice crusted with a golden vine
that lodged among the thick roots of an oak.
This legendary cup whose jeweled light
delibly stains the throat that will invoke
it should be raised to your lips like a bright
sword where your name is etched in brambles of steel
roses and never surrendered, then she
might laugh among the tables and the real
be what is dreamed in the green shade of the tree.

Ursa Major

I

The Spanish archers shot till their arms ached,
quivered their bolts in breast or neck of bear.
Never again would the great grizzlies come
wind rippling fur, to dig the sweet, white roots.
If earth could somehow sense their absent tread,
their paws like hands on a woman's flank, the gold
hills curving leg or hip beneath their bulk,
there would be quakes with fissures that would spill
Los Osos Creek into the brightening meadows
where only in potency their dream exists.
But those born near this place might receive
an intuition of what lingers here
like drifted fur or slashes on a trunk
and long to see furred heads now vague as light.

IV

Those emblematic animals who lived
in this or any other place are not
wind woven in the tapestries of grass
nor are they caught and saved by the golden rune
flashed through a shifting branch but fabulous
still they exert in dreams a murderous pull
from life to death in wishing for what was.
Soon I may never find a bear in a lens
far down the only path to water, fur
riffling like pins beneath a magnet, fear
flooding my veins until I taste the scent
of things that shimmer, swimming through the wind.
Binoculars cased and thumping I would run
into a clearing where he stands, immense,
fetid, fish scales the tiny moons on his coat.

VI

If I took a branch and placed it where the spine
should be and used a coffee can for a skull
and coated these with mud, trying to push
my breath into the holes my fingers made,
into the dirt and sticks and rags for fur,

nostrils would fill with water, black beneath
my lips like poisoned cups I must not drink.
I cannot make this effigy of mud
receive a pulse from correspondent stars
scrawling their vibrant forms across the sky.
I cannot make one rise from meadows red
with poppies, circling flies around his head.
There are no meadows now; condos rise
where grizzly trails would make a man stop once
whisper a prayer and carefully test the wind.

Owl 2

Owl hears whatever moves
and drops through the dark trees
onto the brush he shoves
aside but when the breeze
fans the down on his chest
he rises like a skull
and crossbones—white wings pressed
on a black page—and all
the moonlight concentrates
in his fur, his yellow eyes.
Up in an oak he waits
as the rats squeal and rise
through branches, toward a bark
nest swaying on the trunk.
The mound rides like an ark
but the blunt bow is sunk
in leaves as he comes down
and pulls rats out to drown.
Like Pluton in a world
of dust, owl clearly sees
vague bodies that are whirled
like cloth that turn and freeze
beneath the yellow talons.
If I imagine a place
near the burning pylons
where a white ruined face
must pass, I would see owl blink
somewhere above the stream
of whispers where faces sink
and memory is a dream.

Owl 5

I

A smoking mirror colder than a lake
can spread your face like silver on a wave.
White lips above the swaying waters break
their wings through a dark air which I engrave
with my pale markings though I try to save
myself from all reflection when a crown
of lights winks in the blue and seems to drown.

II

My bathrobe opens in a sudden gust.
Its gray silk puffs around the shoulders—black
lines run down the sleeves, white down at my chest.
I'm at the window, fingers in the crack
where cold air issues as I hunch my back
to lift and see thorn branches whip the air;
wind ruffling the light plumage of my hair.

Wind wearing at the skin of temple and jaw
of the owl who dives into my moonlit yard
and the wings splash on the mouse stuck with straw.
When he rises I think I see eyes starred
like cut glass and I try to disregard
these heavy bones; move like the owl, the shark
of night, and pick whatever is, from the dark.

from
Separate Lives

Phosphor

In a classroom we hold up sheets of music.
We chant in Latin with changing voices.
Because she thinks I am the gentlest
Sister Angela picks me out.
When I can't get the right tone or pitch
she puts her face to my face, "Sing! Sing!"
The wen on her cheek quivers on a skin
so white it almost seems like phosphorous.
I know she'll hit me in a second
but nothing will make me sing now.
It is during moments such as this
that one makes promises to oneself.
I place my hand on the flat of anger's blade
and tell myself I will never again
accept another's violence.
When she banishes me to homeroom forever
I read Newsweeks in the classroom next door
and trace on folding-maps those black arrows
where marines were landing in Inchon.
In daydreams of that war I did not think
of the white fragments glowing, stuck to skin.
But I thought again and again of Angela,
of her metallic skin infused with heat
glowing in my mind like phosphor, or Lucifer,
the morning star erased by a rising sun.

Cloud Trains

"There are foxes as wild and shy as wolves"
who run the rust-scaled tracks but never hear
humming vibrations which predicted once
the sliding tons and tiny faces pressed
to windows bright with cutlery and laughter.

American railroads have abandoned routes
like this—hundreds and hundreds of miles.
There are coyotes, foxes, but no wolves.
There is a landscape rushing through the night,
isolate in memory, a glowing dot.

The drawn-out whistle of a train would reach
through miles and miles where no one would have been.
A marking light seemed distant as a star.
Someone out there would sigh, dog-ear a page,
the light extinguish like a lamp a miner wore.

Pulsations of desire can make a man
an engine scooping tunnels from the dark,
burning and grinding where most of us won't look.
But if red brushes gliding there would catch
a glance, sly interlocaturs would fix

an eye on iron, on lines no longer bright.
They're ruled as straight or curved as the blunt lead
of compasses could draw. They're glazed as blue
as the sky where uncorroded metal still
receives like water whatever passes there.

The sky's motilities, wind-driven clouds,
are brought to earth and no one in a train
seems lonely to a lonely eye that stares
occasionally through focused lenses, where
only the wisps and trails of cloud trains are.

Taped Music

On a hot night when no one slept
an orange moon spread
on the waters somewhere off the Philippines,
sailors propped against the steel bulkheads
played the tapes of women's voices.
They held flashlights and smoothed
wrinkled letters on their thighs.
A night patrol thumped and skidded
across the flight deck below.
They showed each other photos.
Most of the women were not beautiful
but men would nod and gently say, "Beautiful."
A Boatswain's Mate laughed and said, "Whore."
Men punched him so hard and often
blood darkened his dungaree shirt.
There would be letters from Sasebo and Yokosuka
with photos of women in kimonos.
Men would read these letters over and over,
memorizing phrases of awkward English
as though they were passages of poems.
When I asked what made these women different,
there were bitter smiles, someone
said something about divorce,
something about simple things
with these Japanese women.
The great ship turned into a fresh wind
and men slept beneath the stars.
Some mumbled. Some turned
into each other and cursed.
Some dreamed of those who would receive
their desire. Cheeks pressed the rubber matting
of the steel deck plates, arms shielded
the eyes of those who only recently were boys.

The Game Keeper

I drive through the oaks, the heavy brush cut back,
the nettles lightly whipping the windshield.
I emerge in a clearing, and look down through the arch
of shedding leaves glazed with light, into a stand
of redwoods and meadow where deer freeze
before they sprint into the foliage.
An oak branch, knotted like an arm, rests
on the sagging roof of the house where I once lived.
Aunt Kay is gone. Glynn, my cousin, died
a year ago from too much drink.
I remember how we'd sit in the ruined house
with music, lights blazing into the trees,
laughing, drinking, talking about books.
We'd sit in the sun drinking beer,
reading newspapers, novels, magazines
and put them down to argue out of context.
We'd do this at the beginning of the summer
till the awful jobs we had to have came through
and we would set chokers on logs or push
steel cradles into retorts at the cannery.
Now the green creepers push through split casements
and the woods reclaim portions of the meadow.
"Glynn, you lived in the midst of beauty."
But there was blank darkness in his eyes.
He would go still, bite back on the pain
and be somewhere else. I know internal landscapes.
At the end he lived in a blasted field, a charred house.
His delicacy, his musical wit are gone
and the world is a stranger place.
I wander these woods like a game keeper,
or the last scion of a ruined lord.

Poetry Reading
for Don Justice

Beneath his kindness, generosity
and gentleness unusual strength resides.
You barely hear the traces of a drawl
which if you knew such things, would document
his place of birth as Florida or Georgia.
Tonight he reads his poems in a packed hall.
His syllables are cut and polished stones.
I know the long hours, years even, spent
beneath the lamplight pouring over worksheets.
I know the exactions of his art have ground
rough edges like a pumice stone and left
the essence of the man in silences,
in lines and phrases traced onto a page
or the air for those who listen here tonight.
The cause for what we hear can be found only
in the ethos of a man who holds himself
most strictly bound to what is difficult.
After the reading, though we talk, laugh, drink
there is a kind of silence one might find
at the hushed center of a storm, a place
his voice and perfect ear have made for us.
The storm is cold and chaos; it is the world.
But for an hour or so we seem to move
in a charmed circle of protective light,
affection warming us like the good wine.

Tai Chi

Dreaming hands, "cloud hands," drift before him
in a cirrus of skin and feathered silk.
The polished wood is water where he glides.

People in the stands, not knowing what he does,
hush at the mastery of a man who moves
like a swan until his robes are unfurled wings.

I have tried to move this way and be this way
but I have not lived with such singleness
of purpose, such purity of heart.

I'll go into my room, stand with knees bent
hands cupped in front of me and closing my eyes
try to think of nothing or one thing.

Then practice forms in my backyard, inhale,
exhale from the belly up and, rooted, stretch
my joints behind each slow punch, block or kick.

Some morning when the sun's a floating disc,
white in the shielding leaves above I'll move
as though these synchronous and dreaming hands

were emblems of a self united, healed
at last, hands paddling through the tidal air,
every move cut in the glass of a still pond.

There are Photographs

We sat together at a table, all
of us so firmly dedicated we
could think of little else besides a grail
of words in every circumstance an eye
or ear could search. These moments quickly passed.
Now some of those caught there in black and white
have died or disappeared into the vast
crowds thronging the blurred avenues of light.
Even their features in the photographs
yellow or darken or erase themselves
in some locked drawers where the one who laughs
has lost hair, lips and eyes or on some shelves
where obliterating time coats these with dust.
The negatives prove some of us were there
with all we were, our eyes lit by a gust
of light blown from banked candles on the air.
Overexposed, a photo puts a tongue
of flame across the red-oak center board
and there our hands pressed flat as though unstrung
by the toothed flame shaped something like a sword.
Where now are Levis, Trejo, Jones, Spear, all
of those who at this rounded table posed
that day like brothers with a common goal
before the light failed and the shutter closed.

from
Spring Drive

September Winds

The spotted avocado leaves
break loose and flutter down.
Inert as corpses, they pile up
as winds make branches moan.

We give trees extra water, lave
their roots with vitamin-
laced liquids the dogs would drink.
I put a hand's blotched skin

against a leaf half-crushed and find
similitudes I wish
I could ignore another year.
But stemmed leaves harshly clash.

How many things snap loose then sink
in their own ruined stream?
The desiccations of this wind
are merciless as time.

Spring Drive

This language we have often loved too much
constrains us even as we drive through pink
and white orchards, their buds clouding our eyes,
which range from the black lanes to the snow-capped
Sierras in the east. Our syllables
equivocate on the cool streams of air
slipping through windows cracked and open vents.
Some might approximate the colors massed
against the lime-washed trunks, the painted sky.
But most delineate abstractions bare
as branches winter and the wind have stripped.
The vowels our flesh has shaped go out
in decibels oscilloscopes might trace
in white sine waves on green cathode ray tubes.
Recited from a page, they enter ears
which provide portals to another's flesh.
So metrical accents beating like a heart
may replicate in someone else's breast.
At least we hope today this may be true,
on this trip through a valley flooding pink
and white before the fruit spurs tug their stems
toward black soil washed down from the Sierras.
Dust of our flesh will someday merge with the earth
but rises from it now like trees observed.
Tongues rooted in our throats articulate
invisible blossoms on streams of air.

My Pagan Name

When a nun said I had a pagan name,
I shrugged and smiled, thinking of dragon ships,
men with horned helmets, bracelets, and short swords.
They waded through the surf with foaming knees.
She didn't know I had, as patron saint,
a warrior archangel with a flame
sword, breastplate and shield bright as the sun
in those holy cards she gave me when I aced
a test or memorized state capitals.
This wasn't Ireland. No one ever called me
Michael, through red italics driven deep
into my baptismal certificate's
wax-sealed parchment attested to this fact.
My "pagan name" identifies one who
makes gloves, most likely leather carefully stitched
along the fingers and wrists soft as skin.
Good craftsmanship isn't necessarily
a pagan thing, and though I knew the nun
was merely stupid, I would search myself
for any trace of paganism, wild
as air-whirled spume from shocked waves on rocks.
I dreamed of gauntlets lacing steel with gold.
Much later, I would wonder what's in a name
if it can't indicate some essence or
some vaguely apprehended quality
obliquely glimpsed in several dreams before
brought finally into being by an act.
At last may my emergent self, moon-bright,
cut like a disc through all-obscurant clouds.
My pagan name is like a second skin
provided by a glove and easily peeled
when molting is necessity and the fist
must show its row of knuckles, pale and hard.

A Navy Pilot's Wife

She knew her husband would buzz
the house when his squadron
flew back from the carrier.
A Zero waggled its wings.
Its pilot may've thought
she was a spy or the white
cloths were surrender flags.
She pinned them on the line
until the first explosions
blossomed far below
and the anchored fleet
began to burn. A few guns cut loose and there
were sirens, loudspeakers, bells.
She sprinted for her door
and that was her story.

Something about this always
appealed to my mother,
my aunt and other women
who listened to this tale
of a mother oblivious
for a moment to all
the possibilities
of bombs and cannon shells,
great, flammable lakes
of aviation fuel.
All of them admired
this woman flaunting rags
at martial power even
if this act seemed absurd,
or seemed like an unconscious
slip asserting powers
of life, reminding us
there's no man who did not
once wear his own stained rags.

Young Sailors on Liberty

Sometimes on Saturdays they'd hitch hike south
to Washington, D.C. There they could drink
beer at eighteen in the jazz clubs and mouth
sweet notes a trombone's neon sliding sank
into the darkest places they could feel.
And those immoral, fabled women who
worked for the government might slowly trail
them, after closing, street glazed blue
or red by pulsing signs and gentle rains.
If they could reach the park where monuments
dropped columns on the pools that shivered pines,
why, anything could happen in the dense
shadows of all that foliage charged with dew.
But usually nothing came of this, and sailors,
like chained-up animals in the park zoo,
howled, drank till headlights of passing cars
merged with other lights. Then they, with arms
entwined, like men surviving battle, limped
homeward toward a cheap hotel. Perhaps the worms
of their desire, anesthetized, lay slumped
at last in alcohol, bathed by the tides
in all those bottles tilted toward their lips.
Some slept, a wrist above their eyes; their needs,
submerged, ran swiftly in their blurring shapes.

Dark Corridors

Antidotes for nerve gas coated his joints,
and now he needs another career.
He'd like to teach and write. He's twenty-nine.
His name's Jeff. He has a reddish-brown mustache,
light blue eyes. He's tanned. He seems fit,
but his joints ache when he sinks into a chair,
gripping the edges of my desk, tightening his mouth.

He knelt on a sand dune and spoke
precise coordinates into a hand-held radio.
The circling fighter bombers blew apart
Iraqi artillery, SPCs, and bunkers.
Like a biblical angel, he pointed, and blasts
of light left scorched metals, burned rags, and rocks.
After this, columns of our tanks and trucks pushed
into the perpetual darkness
of burning oil fields.
                    Figures lit, sometimes by flames,
sometimes by truck headlights wandered there
in bandages and pain till MPs made
them kneel and bound their wrists with plastic cuffs.

Jeff sighs telling me things like this,
then rises on his ruined joints, thanks me
and slowly moves down darkened corridors.

Letter to my Brother

I'll visit someday soon, sit on the beach
with you at Todos Santos drinking beer.
We'll raise quart bottles of Pacifico
and swear, "This is the life," and know it isn't.
We'll claim the pressures of our lives up north
dissolve in Mexico; but we both know
I will grow too restless in a day or two.
I'll pack and drive the molten highway north
through land so starkly cut from rocks and dunes
it seems a sculptor's hand went everywhere.
But I'm describing what I've never seen
unless it was that day when a friend and I,
driving south, crossed at Tecate, drove east
through desert flats until we reached the Gulf.
The hills beyond the town were carved black rock.
It was San Felipe's day, and all streets
were filled with colors, blouses, banners, red,
white, green, on cardboard booths that blocked the streets.
I sat with Milton Savage at a booth
with planks for seats and watched the bikers come
and go at a cantina just across the street.
As Milton drained a pitcher, his red beard
flecked with foam. A man in colors sat
beside him, said, "We'll take this town apart,
take anything we want. So be with us."
He pointed at the Harleys, packed in ranks
in front of swinging double doors that broke
the raucous waves of laughter and the shouts.
The vendor, hearing this, put someone else
in charge, walked quickly down the crowded street.
It took full half an hour before we heard
the tramp of combat boots, and saw a platoon
of carabiñeros in battle-dress
approach the yellow cantina where all
the music and shouting seem to be.
A sergeant shouted, "*A la derecha.*"
Soldiers aligned themselves in perfect ranks.
He shouted something else and their right hands
reached for green sheaths and drew their bayonets

I saw along an upper lip thin beads
of sweat and a light tremor in the hands
of the young rifleman. An officer drew
his pistol, held it at his side, and strolled
into the bar; then men spilled out and kick-
started their bikes, gunned them until they roared,
their forearms quivering as they left that town.
We said together, *"Viva Mexico,"*
and raised our foaming glasses to the sun,
Milton and I, like brothers under arms.

Wild Parrots

Glancing down a lane
dappled with sunlight slanting
through the high leaf banks,
he sees the branches quivered
by a flock of wild parrots
people inadvertently released.
These gorgeous birds, green with orange
throats or blue throats or purple
beaks that flew into the fruit trees
and ate some peaches or figs,
learned they could live on their own.
Every year he sees a flock,
larger, more obstreperous
scolding the cats and dogs,
flying north or south,
wherever they go for the rest
of the year when he'll forget
them or think occasionally
of a raucous joy he'd never
seen before or since.
As they rise defiantly, they
let slip a memorized
word or two, broken
syllables flowing back
over their wings into the past
as though parrots would deprecate
our Adamic power to fix
things in a place with names.

I Wasn't There

When they murdered Charles Cunningham, my first
best friend, I was five hundred miles north
of The Aztec Drive-in Theater where they found
him on his knees leaning on a metal stand,
face white as painted speakers dotting the acres
like markers at Normandy or Arlington.
Charles might have smiled a little, licked his lip.
He may've thought some adolescent insult
or challenge was an act until he closed
with two of them, whoever they were, and a blade
slid into him and twisted toward his heart.
I have an alibi. I wasn't there
to stand beside him as the huge screen took
the colors broken from a beam of light
and painted heroes up in front of him.
I would've been asleep at my cousin's house.
Oaks, redwoods, pines, the great horned owl and deer
rustled around me all that night as Charles'
blood pooled beneath him on the asphalt where
he knelt before some stupid melodrama.
An usher caught him in a flashlight beam,
then gently shook a shoulder, touched his throat.
But there was nothing anyone could do
for Charles Cunningham.

The Typographer

On days so cold even plumes of breath
returning to your lungs would hurt, we'd move across
the campus cutting through the long buildings
that were kept heated, half-lit even late
into the night, down glossy corridors
past classrooms, offices with frosted glass.
We'd reach a double door, sprint through raw air
to the next building, finally reach the town's
main street and come at last to a warm bar
pulsing with laughter, smoke, and jukebox songs.

One night as I passed by the printing lab,
I glimpsed through a window Harry Duncan's head
clouded with white hair, his hands firm on the wheel,
which, turning, pressed perfectly stationed rows
of inked letters into the blanks of Hosho.
I stopped to watch him circle misspelled words
and other errors as, without looking,
his left hand roved a case of fonts, plucked out
the requisite letters and, once again,
he brought the huge plates down to press a soft,
expectant page with darkening syllables.
Like an Irish monk in a scriptorium,
obedient to the exactitudes,
silently bent over a manuscript
he would illuminate, Duncan displayed
more care and belief than I'd ever seen
from anyone as he worked through those nights.

Luxuria

after Prudentius

When she appeared, her white robe stained by wine
spilling from her cupped hand onto the oak
floor near our beds, we would not think we were
trapped in a dream, especially when she tugged
her sash, purpling it where her fingers touched.
It flowed past one knee poking through the cloth.
We had trained hard all day, running through sand,
holding our rifles at high port in swamps,
creek water up to our armpits at times.
Before we slept, we polished all the parts
and stacked our useless rifles in gun racks.
We were as strong as we would ever be,
but, oh God, in this dream we were like deer
caught in a headlight's beams, when she at last
came sliding at us through balsam and wine.
Behind her, chariots crusted with gems
rocked slightly in a wind that seemed to trail
her fluttering robe, held shut with one slim hand.
Then on the marble of a throat as smooth
and white as anything we'd ever seen,
the fires of variegated gem-lights played.
We were young men and our desires had made
us vulnerable to the blandishments
a lovely woman easily employs.
The chariot wheels with their electrum rims
encircling polished spokes began to flash
a whitening succession of silver rays
against the barrack's walls into our eyes
as we lay stunned on our disheveled bunks
like men whose wounds smoked on a darkening field.
She said, "I am not pleasure, I am pain."

Sleeping Woman
for Chaim Soutine

She seems so vulnerable with her brown
hair spread in coils and loops against the white-
blue pillowcase, and too much like a girl
with her receding chin, mascara smeared,
lipstick smudged, eye shadow much too thick.
Her lips are parted as she breathes and sighs,
and her neck's plunged into a blouse so red
the painter must have loaded up his brush.
Some of it streaks the cup where her throat meets
breast bone, where her right hand, half-closed, has come
to rest as though it could protect her heart.
The lid of her right eye comes halfway down
to a straight line painted white as a scar:
It splits the pupil lurking under it,
keeping its watches where her dreams commence
above the bar where she must work most nights.
A slip of the hand put brown just above
her head, a brush stroke straying from her blouse
makes a red slash on her hair; all of this
creates a sense of a life's rough textures,
mystery more vivid now than what was real.

The Jeweler

My great-grandfather packed his best suitcase
and left behind his lyrical Cymri
for a glittering jewelry store in Canada.
Wheels, springs, and intricate gears would click beneath
his hands and, for a while, beat like a heart.
Diamonds he tapped along a scored line broke
in perfect angles, light refracting blue,
white, red like polished blades against the sun.
Talent and a long apprenticeship gave him
such mastery he could do anything
jewelers might want to do with pendants, pearls,
engravings etched in gold, or the brass-bound
chronometers on a ship's quarterdeck.
Eventually he'd own a jewelry store
in London, Ontario, and earn so much
he'd speculate in stocks and bonds. He bought
some fields near Houston for grapefruit, then sold
them just before oil spouted from a drill.
We framed his picture set in a collage
with other relatives now gone forever.
We hung it on our dining room's pink wall
where gradually it fades like some of the myths
an American family would maintain
a generation or two, claiming roots,
distinction, some small part in destiny.

But where are the Welsh battle hymns, the poems
whose syllables are set in tight form
like polished stones in a bracelet's web?
Where is the power to dream prophetic dreams
bequeathed by Merlin's gold-dust words scattered
to every quarter of a ragged map?
Somewhere descendants blink back particles
of light or loose a diamond in a tear.

Descent

Shellacked in place below a dented skull
two femurs move a little as though cramped
in the cut-down wooden case my uncle holds.
Beneath a sheet of plastic, clear as glass,
glossed yellow bones are spotting lincoln-green.
They seem to swim beneath my Uncle John's
spatulate fingers as he says, "This is art."
He is thin and shabby now in his loose clothes.
He seems to've lost all that fierce dignity
and bite that frightened us when we were boys.
We step inside the basement door and pull
it shut with knotted rags attached to pegs.
And dust is everywhere and everything.
A swaying staircase rises toward a door,
edges ajar, light-lined in reddish gold.
We rise towards music from a radio,
the murmuring voices from the distant rooms.
When I push through at last, my uncle's gone,
and I am helpless in a world of light.
But even dreaming this, I know that dawn's
obliterating tides of consciousness
will soon return, flooding with its own light
a fading parlor with some relatives
who, bending, gently say the kind of things
one says to babies or to animals.

Burial Dream

All through the yard the dried weeds grew waist-high,
speckled with aphids, locusts and huge fleas.
I should've cut and sprayed a month ago.
I thought I heard the power mower whine.
When I peeked around the corner of the shed,
I saw my father, dead now eleven months,
cutting wide circles near the lemon trees.
I'd call to him but knew he couldn't hear.
But when I blinked and he was gone, I noticed
someone had knocked some boards from the back fence,
torn loose the covering chicken wire. When I
came close, I found a doe wedged there, two legs
stiffening in the air, throat ripped out by dogs.
Already flies were clustering on the wound.
They hummed like a downed power line, green and black
and glistening in a liquid light that seemed
to pour from her huge eyes. Before her stench
began to fill the yard, I'd have to dig a hole
downhill and break her stiff legs in;
pile stones on dirt to keep the coyotes
from digging up the corpse and scattering bones.
But she was heavy and her brown fur stained
as it came loose and stuck to my right palm.
I had to turn my head and pull the body
down the hillside, then drive my mattock down
into decomposed granite, spooning up
red earth so there could be a burial.
I'd bury in this dream more than a doe
dog-slaughtered on my fence's wire and wood.
I'd cover the old grievances like snow
falling all afternoon on distant hills,
stretching clear to a landlocked, frozen sea.

from
My Cap of Darkness

My Cap of Darkness

1.
A photo in a yearbook catches me
as I lean nonchalantly on a green
bleacher, not posing, cradling a helmet,
paint streaked from collisions with running backs.
And I remember, how on several
occasions, the whole world went dark
as our heads butted with a crack, gold lights
twinkling on the black velvet of the sky.
For a moment, this helmet was a cap
of darkness without the capabilities
Perseus possessed, letting him move
unseen among various enemies.
If I could move invisibly among
those who discuss my life, my work
I would unsheathe a head whose serpentine locks hiss
and strike the air above my trembling hand
turning to stone the minds of those who think
they see my inner darknesses where gaps
of deprivation yawn, widening as they watch.

2.
Oh day of anger, when eyelids must fall
like curtains rippling down, and the vague spot
at the back of my skull, where a vein blew
apart, no longer buzzes when the low
pressures elicit thunderheads and bolts
riving the clouds with their white, jagged scars.
Then I will feel my cap of darkness pull
too tightly down, and I won't see or move
loose among the crowds on boulevards,
malls, parking lots—wherever my countrymen
would gather; and I'll know the time is near
when I won't hear spadefuls of dirt drum down
on a wood lid locked just above my head.

3.
Then sleep—until the day gold trumpets blare
hoping you will feel then, your bones recoat

92

with skin, and some fresh blood flow through your veins
somehow reconstituted, as loose dirt
drifts from your hair and shoulders, everything
suddenly bright, pure air in your new lungs.
Then rip your cap of darkness loose and stand
waiting with muscular ease for what must come.

Bear Song

James Welch and I were very drunk.
   He got down on all fours
chanting a Blackfoot brown bear song.
   Wind nudged the kitchen doors.

Dizzily we swayed on the rough tiles
   reddening beneath our knees
and did not see the moon's effects
   glowing through the banked trees.

We grunted, rolling our bleared eyes,
   glancing at our bare arms
as though a thick fur sprouted there
   invoked by magic charms:

bear teeth and claws threaded by chains,
   formations of firebirds
painted on Jim's sport shirt, the smoke
   of sweet grass mixed with words.

The family cat pushed through and stopped.
   His fur stood up like quills
and then he streaked through the back yard
   on grass where the moon spills

herself continuously through
   a bodice's ripped silk,
black against a bare white skin.
   Some spots seemed drenched with milk.

Hyperostosis

Bone spurs were forming up and down his spine.
He could no longer bend way down to pick
up litter in his yard or lace his shoes
or easily swivel his neck left or right.
His vertebrae were casing themselves in bone
as though his skeleton inherited
armor to ward off life's inevitable blows.

Some Celtic ancestors too often bore
the shock of battle-car collisions, axe
against the helm, shield or leather casing thighs.
Somehow, over time, they printed in their genes
compensatory templates which became
a malady descendants must endure.
An x-ray photo shows a white haze spread
from bones around his neck and down his back.

Oh, let this man now move more fluidly
in his stiff cage of bones, remembering how
he once was agile as a dancing bear.
And let him have his cap of darkness so
he can move invisibly among all those
who thought he would be ineffectual
because of sorrow, age and this disease,
the gorgon which would paralyze him now.

Surgery

The surgeons whispering above would give
him a titanium and cobalt hip.
Perhaps the pain-muffling anesthesia let
some things rise from their unconscious sources.
But light from the burning lamps seemed to congeal
into flocked gold—orchards, plowed fields, a horse
all carved into a cathedral door ajar,
trembling as though it might soon disappear.
He longed to rise, push through and talk to those
whose faces made vague lines against the light,
flowing through the bright jambs and on the side
where something like the wind half opened it.
He did not see the angel ether induced
when he was six and Doctor Warner cut
his tonsils out in a downtown office.
He saw this golden space whose entrance might
require his death and that which makes him live
would have to rise from his splayed body, left
seeking the splendor of a light-carved door.

My Late Wife's Clothes

There's a faint odor of her skin on bright
cloth she cut, stitched and wore against the sun
like primordial emblems of the beautiful.
If only a strong wind would fill these clothes
I'd stand out in the cold and once again
I would admire the gently curving hips,
and the black straps resting on shoulders where
my hands would light like falcons on a perch.
I'd cup them in both hands and gently pull
her toward me, lips lingering on fragrant skin.
I touch a sweater red as blood which I
once wrapped in tissue, placed beneath the tree
she decorated with strung tinsel, bulbs,
gold angels with our names engraved on wings.
I want to shut the door and leave this room;
do anything but bundle up her clothes.

Terminalia

Oh God, we're animals bearing this gift
of tongues, thinking and dreaming, knowing more
than we should, bodies faltering year by year,
some new event erupting like a sore.

And though the syllables our mouths have shaped
could snare its essence with a perfect name
this act would temporarily end our powers
leaving the tribulation much the same.

And when the relevant discovery comes,
at last, it comes too late for most of us,
struggling through roughened currents which our lives
provide until we reach pale terminus.

Virtue

for Palmer Hall

"Leave it all on the field," our football coach
once said, our cleats clicking on the cement
locker room floor before we trotted out
onto a field chalk-lined beneath the ranked
floodlights where huge moths butted the hot spheres.
Tonight the field for Palmer is a room
reserved for readings, rows of folding chairs
packed with colleagues who seemed to focus all
their listening energies on this man's words,
his poems and essays as he stands and speaks
into a microphone, fighting the urge
to sway and tremble with his afflictions.
Such fortitude is what the Romans called
virtue, taking it from their word for man.
His right hand shaking just a little, he
stills it by an effort of his will and sounds
out syllables as though they are the notes
inked on a score which is his life tonight
and always; let us remember how he stands
bracing his voice against a malign wind.

An Old Man in Sunlight

Sitting in the sunlight, falling asleep,
he dreams of ink blots swirling on the blue.
Murder of crows go caw, caw as they sweep
down, black flags folding, some of them askew.
These semaphores have jolted him awake.
Rising, he curses then back into flight,
raucous complaints issuing from every beak.
Splashed syllables and feathers streak the white
air black, making it seem as though this were
just one more canvas of those things stretched
across his memory. So let him blur
in sleep whatever hurtful scenes have etched
their fluent lines as though a human brain
were copper, stone, paper with a flocked grain.

Pulsar

Now let what you have hurt
emit no piercing cry
like the exhausted bat
I crushed. And where he lay
on the white sill, as flat
as a t-shirt emblem
pressed onto cloth by an iron,
a stain shaped like a stem
leaked from his lips. No siren
summoned a blood-drunk host
from cellar, eave or cave.
He would dip, dart and coast
above, trying to save
himself from my broom, swung
over and over through
the air till his tongue hung
like a dog's tongue but blue
when he lit on the sill, his
impeccable radar
making him invincible
till then. But there's a pulsar
of agonizing cries,
to which this creature might
contribute as he dies,
pressed beneath his fright
and a book on the broom straw.

Poppies

for Richard Diebenkorn

A glass of water on a table top
as gray as slate contains four poppy stems
and these erect their paper-thin orange cups.
Paint darkened at their centers makes two vague
shapes, one's something like a dove with spread wings,
the other looks like a broken hourglass.
Perimeters are lighter where it seems
the artist mixed more yellow in his paint.
A black floor frames the table with these stripes
vertically running down to the table's edge
but interrupted there. These stripes offset
a little to the canvas center's right.
I have no idea what these represent.
But the stripes may indicate Diebenkorn used
the golden section to compose this piece.
He has proportioned space so that a slight
imbalance may establish in the eye
of the beholder a residual sense
of movement pleasing to a restless mind
whose hot flaws turn it like a molten ball.
One glowing poppy breaks the white, red stripes
before they reach the slate the blue has touched.
There's no true stasis in anything alive.

Wayne Tiebaud's Cakes

bear frostings red, tan, yellow, white or green
and the brush strokes are not more evident
than swirling textures bakers would have squeezed
from decorating tubes onto moist decks.
Another painting has depicted cakes
halved and their inner sections lined with dark
chocolate, but yellow as stucco in between.
I might slice through such decorated shapes
without regard for what Tiebaud has done
appropriating pleasure of taste to sight.

There was a huge sheet cake two of us slid
into the back of Lyle's old panel truck.
He had mixed food dyes with whipped cream, squirted them
onto a rough template of a bride and groom.
He printed letters, birds, bright numerals.
He stepped back sighing, cocked his head then made
some tiny changes and the whole two yards
of cake became a vivid-rough tableau.

Driving downhill we hit a bump and the cake
split as though a fissure from a quake
on a snow field decapitated bride
and groom and smudged red icing on a bird;
a line of text had broken from his beak.
I stared at the disaster right behind
us, as Lyle said "it'll be okay," and took
out his containers of whipped cream, his box
of implements, redrew the heads of bride
and groom, smoothed fissures with his spatula.

If Lyle saw Tiebaud's paintings he might say
"at least my cakes are real," and few could blame
this baker with all his practical skills.
But much of what we liked about Lyle's cakes
was their adornment, figures, colors, texts
demolished in a minute by our forks.

Fresno's Underground Gardens

On Sundays men from C street strolled across
the baked dirt, hard pan running down five feet
beneath it, they would descend into the earth
down the steps Baldasare cut from stones.
They'd tug a bell rope and he'd scuttle down
a tunnel and appear unchaining gates
so these Italian laborers could work
with him awhile, then drink some wine, play cards
in a plaza still shaded by his trees
whose branches poked through a dome carved from rock
and shaped so that heat circled through the hole
where oranges, grapefruit, lemons dot the blue.
They worked in the San Joaquin Valley's heat
trenching for new gas lines or putting up
telephone poles they'd soaked in creosote
for days so that corrosive oils would coat
their gloves and burn the soft skin under eyes
when one or two of them forgot and wiped
away the sweat coursing in runnels down
their faces, chests, and backs, blue work shirts damp.
Antonio Maggori, Joe Maduano
would rest in these cool depths, arms coiled like steel
wire braided cable when they reached across
the rock slab table for more bread and wine.
And you might see them ranged on either side
of Baldasare in black and white photos
superimposed on other ones tacked up near
the entrance to this place where briefly
he presides like Pluton in this underworld.
Oh let these men return in the springtime
when the earth's fecund powers assert themselves
pushing all manner of living things through crusts
broken into the light and vivid air.

Beneath the Mission Walls

I love the thick, adobe walls, the red
tile floors roughened by years of sandals, shoes
boots shuffling over them and the enclosed
courtyard where flowers planted in squares and circles
suggest an influence of Spain's Arab
architects who built in fluid stone
gorgeous geometries of eternity.
Year after year returning to this place
I dig through memory beneath these walls
as though my shambling presence bulked by age
could find some nourishing substance here where
my mother, aunts and uncles knelt beneath
a choir loft braced by large, rough-hewn beams.
I stand where Spanish archers must have stood
before they shot their bolts into the fur
of grizzlies digging for the sweet, white roots
which once grew just beneath the bank's black earth.

Revolt

If our oaks coughed the way sick men
   cough there'd be tiny dust
clouds where folds in the bark make lips
   and where sap forms a crust.

There'd be no syllables when stuck
   lips parted and no tongue
within to shape the sounds a tree
   might make unless wind-stung

branches lash and sing, some torn
   loose, littering the ground.
But let one oak lean forward, snap
   white rootlets all around,

step tentatively like a child
   learning how to walk,
its tall trunk tottering, a place
   for saws marked with blue chalk.

This might signal the trees' revolt
   against our ordinances
as the parched leaves articulate
   in flames their grievances.

Song for Renewal

After four years of drought rain comes
at last ticking on the skylight,
washing the dusty, half dead oaks,
and the interminable blight.

Grasses on my hillside are gold.
Sluicing their dust the boulders gleam.
Because of this spring flowers may sprout
again beside our dried up stream.

Let water gently flow downstream,
the mule deer bend to drink once more
but moderate rain's turbulence,
all manner of living things restore.

A Small Town

Because the air in this small Texas town
is soft and pure and leaves no grains of soot
on limestone blocks exposed a hundred years
or so, I think I could live here someday.
I'd spot an Airstream trailer on a lot
not far from the town's center, stroll downtown,
drink coffee with old men my age who might
wear silver buckles won in rodeos
but tarnished now; they'd push back Stetsons creased,
sweat-dark along the brim, with scuffed up boots
beneath them as they murmur through the summer heat.
I'd compare this place to the red-dotted towns
on California maps, their Spanish names;
San Luis Obispo, Mariposa, Fresno.
There'd be a man who'd raise his coffee cup
into a beam of light where I could see
an anchor stenciled on sun-darkened skin,
which webs a thumb to a bent finger—flukes
blue as sea water in those Mason Jars
holding dead specimens boys kept too long.
The tattoo's colors wash back into skin.
Mesquite, brown grasses rippling in the wind,
and the white sand out on the burning plains
blurred his eyes though dark glasses shielded them
as he rode down the strays he'd rope and brand.
Perhaps this speculation has its source
in movies or T.V. and then perhaps
no one in such a place would easily talk
to me or any stranger walking in.

Wild Music

for Mariana

We will return, my love, to this small town.
Where the Alsatian houses glow pale blue
or white with metal roofs which slope down toward
fenced-in plots crammed with vines, wild grasses, flowers
rioting against some weathered planks. There are
bluebonnets and red poppies cupping flames
in cell-phone photographs you took the day
I posed against the splotched, raw colors there.
I would have picked a red bouquet for you
but a dog lurking near waited for one
of us to touch his planks where blossoms scored
the wood like painted notes on blown parchment.
No Irish monk would emulate these staves
for any illuminated manuscript.
But loving their rough textures I would play
them, wondering what wild music I could spill
on the air and if they might give us a song
like a tune plucked from an Aeolian Harp,
wind in the strings, wind in your wheat-gold hair.

The River Walk

A bank of lilies may reflect white scrolls
onto the river's marbled-green which rilled
by breezes rocks them in a wake, unrolls
their rippling parchments, letting the sun-chilled
runes briefly print vague capitals of light.
Such dazzling appearances might mean
nothing despite a fluency of white
dots, dashes foaming on the river's glassine
exterior, angelic texts which none
of us will read or ever comprehend.
And if eternity's graved colophon
crushes beneath a foot as leaves descend
one would still search the river bank to find
it trembling on the margins of the wind.

The Neoteric Poets

When power-drunk generals decided things
they massed their cohorts in a city square.
Anyone trying to stop them could be "proscribed."
You'd see his head impaled on an iron spike,
and this is how they murdered Cicero.
The Republic died forever on that day.

The unnamed Emperor might take his seat
with other senators but they all knew
wherever he might sit would be a throne.
Because of this the Neoteric Poets
retreated to their gardens; there would be
few patriotic poems, no epics till
Virgil composed the Aeneid despite
himself but instructed his heirs to burn
it when he died.
                    Virgil, Propertius
Horace and Catullus all believed they should
concentrate on details: "Keep your sheep fat
and your lines thin."
                    We are so much like them,
carding our lives for things we'd weave like wool
into the lines we station on a page.
Disgusted by our governments, puerile and corrupt,
we will concern ourselves with little things
surrounding us in the green shadows, moist
from watering like the blossoms just beyond us
in patches of light swaying on their stems.

Above it All

Mists rise from my front meadow where the oak
branches obscure whatever lies far down
these hills in the flat valley where the truck
lights blurring spread their cotton on the air.
Whirring down ninety-nine like freight trains run
off broken tracks they suddenly appear
as ghost trains, sometimes ramming slower cars.
You can hear whirlwinds their power generates
before they pass you like something right out
of hell, these burnished battle cars with scythes,
death heads, doors pin-striped with confederate flags.
So I'll stay home until the sun burns through
and perched like an eagle up above it all
in my hilltop home where the air remains
pure and I can look down for miles and miles.
When the sun comes out at last the lit cars flare
and disappear as they race towards the coast.
But from my vantage point I nod above
my yellow legal pads and clouds of sleep
puff from my mind as I try to wield my pen.

I think of the Iliad and Mitchell's new
translation where the Seasons gently strip
gold bridles from White Horses of the sun,
feeding and stabling them near Mount Ida
as Lord Zeus reclines upon a cloud,
ignoring blood-choked mouths, death-dusted eyes
and corpses piled up near the Scaaen Gates.
Though he naps now, he previously took
pleasure from mingling, sometimes disguised, sometimes
invisible with mortals who must die
"clattering to earth in gleaming armor"—brains,
chests, livers pierced with arrows, blades, spear-points.
He loved to toy with them, favoring one side
and then the other as the battle moiled
across the beaches close to the black ships.
And all the lesser gods were even more
mischievous, like Hera who would beg
Aphrodite to help her seduce Zeus,

112

distracting him when Hector needed help,
and Poseidon, who rose from the sea to shake
the earth and aid his faltering Argives.

And even now do similar powers sweep
over and around us, invisible
as the winds driving blue Pacific swells?
Could they determine human destinies,
altering our passages through time and space?
Homer would think so. I don't want to know.
And though I have observed things from these heights,
when the right time comes I'll move into a world
below where things can be touched, tasted, heard
and try to be as solid as a house,
strong as a horse, white blazings on the throat—
at least in vivid dream-fueled reveries—
but finally only a mortal, aging man.

New Poems

Academy of Dreams

Three rows of desks stand
with tan paddle-shaped arms
where children's elbows lean

and bracing hands cup chins
stilling the nodding heads
when way too many words

spill from reddened lips
and sunlight glazes planks
white beneath loose feet.

A wind from nowhere makes
pages in front of them
riffle and breathe like lungs

impaired and some ink bleeds
onto their other hands
obliterating words

which may have created
initial passages
in wisdom's latest text.

Too often dawn whites out
truths demonstrated by
an academy of dreams.

A Father's Dream

My hungry son goes wandering through a mall
past tables loaded with sardine tins, wine,
cheeses with orange rinds, artisanal breads.
He has no money but he runs his hands
across these foods before he disappears
in surging crowds which replicate his bright
blue shirt, their faces turning when I call
his name but every one of them goes blank
as a white page with nothing inscribed there.
Days later my niece tells me he assumed
his wife's last name on his own manuscripts
as if he could erase propinquities
of blood like cursives penciled on a pad
but not inked capitals a letterpress
may drive so deeply in a page one might
begin to hear the stationed syllables
tick beneath a finger running down
a page like echoes from a beating heart.

A Poet's Work

Because towns disappear from my mind's map
I try to summon up things as they were.
Push down on a forefinger paper sliced,
red dots will blot the pages of a map.
But follow it on highway ninety-nine
past towns where plywood shuttered doors are
eyes graying blind beneath their flaking skin.
I remember a time, a man, a voice
whose syllables invoked from clouds of dust
infused with silica stripped from crushed rock,
adobe walls, plaster from ripped drywall,
pain's music rippling into song.
But he has travelled to a dark silence
to a place Dante's meters and rhymes marked,
circles where someday most of us must rest.

Watching a Train Go By

Dreaming some huge, incomprehensible words
a man who'd be an artist made them writhe
on boxcars flashing by us as we wait.
One blood tipped consonant cuts like a scythe,

others are crushing loops the vowels print
on metal roughened by heat and flecked oils.
He'd trace smoke flowing back from the engine,
wielding his spray cans, making fat, gray coils.

His public art, as flawed as it might be,
perhaps drew energy from a desire
for rituals whose painted symbols are
smoke swirling from a brief, oracular fire.

A Writer at Night

Some manuscripts cased in a skull
might slightly riffle, wedged
though they are, between the thickest bones
their uncut pages edged

gold, deckled by light leaked through lids
beneath a mask knocked askew
by restless dreaming hands—dark
pupils turning blue.

He dreams tissues of a brain can be
pages where letters run
blood print pulsing as they describe
what he's done or not done.

In sudden floodings of the light
a nervous hand may serve
as evidence spiritual wounds
inflame a throbbing nerve.

Setting Forth

A ghostly line of sailors all in white
jumpers with sweat-damp circles under arms
salute the flag and one by one request
permission to come aboard. They'll disappear
among the wraith-like fighter bombers, wings
folded above them like protective arms
a dreamer in a nightmare might have raised.
Eighteen, nineteen, twenty they move across
those steel thresholds into another world
the way I did once when I was eighteen,
my hair streaked blond instead of white, my legs
as firm as oaks now rooted in my fields.
For a few weeks or so everything seemed
as exciting as adventures boys might seek.
The desolation of those days at sea
without war, with nothing much to do except
test some capacitors, resistors, bright
arrays of tubes, a doppler radar's bird-
like squeaks as it recorded landing speeds
became what I'd expunge from memory.

Years later walking down the waterfront
I find the Midway anchored near a dock.
Ropes thicker than a man's waist wind around
black bollards glossed by paint a Boatswains's Mate
applied with the same kind of brushes used
on steel deck plates, bulkheads, gun turrets.
I notice harbor waters rippling red,
blue, green reflected from adjacent towers
tonight as though a modern artist strobed
electric neon paints that few would see.
But in the morning tourists lining up
climb gangways to the hanger deck the way
I did once with a seabag crammed with boots,
dress blues, gloves, dungarees, white jumpers, belled
pants, a peacoat, my shaving gear, white hats,
a book or two, skivvies, my spit-shined shoes.
My seabag's bruising heft now prints itself

on my right shoulder in my dreaming mind
with all those sweltering acres, blue and green
stretching to South Pacific horizons.

Grand Canyon

I hoped I'd never dream of these great heights
and falling, flailing my unfettered arms
until the abrupt stop and consciousness
turning into a mist a risen sun
would soon evaporate above some flesh
and splintered, blood-smeared bones, a caved-in skull.
I cautiously approach the rim and peer
into such depths I have to brace myself
against the railing, back away despite
the pastel streaks and other gorgeous tints
on sandstone where the wind and water cut
deeper and deeper through millenniums.
I live again the day I had to climb
the electronic mast of the U.S.S. Midway.
It almost grazed the Golden Gate when we
steamed under it into the Pacific's waves,
blue green, flecked white as our blunt bow cut through.
From time to time I think of the slow climb
up metal steps as I grip the looped wire
handle on a full can of sloshing paint
and later watch paint spill and separate
like rain drops or black tears down the steep chasm
of the air onto the swaying dock below.

A Game of Chess

In the U.S.S. Midway's electronic shop
we'd spend our midwatch hours bent above
chess boards until we got a frantic call.
When banks of radar repeaters lost strobes,
we'd rouse technicians from their triple stacked
bunks so they could then re-illuminate
a glowing abstract version of the sky
above our battle group.
                        Through the long night hours
we'd play until Goldberg yawned and stretched, bored
by his swift victories, my queens toppled
my kings check-mated in a few quick moves.

But one night he told me about a park
in Brooklyn where some relatives and friends
bending above their shuttling pieces tried
to execute intricate strategies inscribed
in the Torah or star-projected lines.
Despite himself he then began to teach
optimal sequences of development.
From that time on I gradually maneuvered
with increasing skill until months later I
would challenge his supremacy from time
to time, my knights escalating havoc
as they ranged rapidly on checkered boards.

At these late hours we fought our drowsiness
but when the games got close Goldberg's brow creased,
a tremor in his voice, his right hand shook
a little as he drew it back and paused,
pondering the problems posed by my black knights.
He'd then begin to extricate his queen
and castle to protect a king in peril.
Eventually he'd withstand horse head knights
vaulting his other pieces, hooking right
and left in an L shaped pattern a sword
arm would have made hacking through flesh and bone.
Watching him I imagined sitting near
Talmudic scholars in a Brooklyn park

leaf shadows mottling beards and the cupped hands
beneath chins as symbolic violence raged
across their boards and leaves like ashes fell.

War Games

I must have been four or five when soldiers
who were recently promoted gave me
some of their obsolete chevrons along
with shoulder patches on which wild cat claws
raked cloth and stitched rivulets on green
or khaki sleeves above the numerals
for the eighty first infantry division.

The Germans had surrendered but our war
in the Pacific went raging on and on.
Men from divisions raised in eastern states
daily arrived at the train station till
Camp San Luis expanded and circled
our town with marching men and tents, trucks, tanks.
Somehow some of the wives managed to knock
on my grandmother's door asking to rent
a room so they could see their husbands one
last time before men filed on board troop trains
bound for Oakland, the gray ships anchored near.
I remember accompanying some wives
to the station where men I liked would lean
from troop train windows fighting back a tear
or two, a few of their lips trembling white.

For years I'd wonder what became of these men
and I'd have daydreams where I'd be with them
clutching a rifle with a fixed bayonet
on a hillside or in a field where grain
hissed in a summer wind with mortar shells
and these were games the boys I knew would play
over and over till the war ended.
But much later I would read about
Okinawa and picture these same men
cut in half or blinded, mutilated
as they went up Mount Suri beside
the First Marine Division, and I thought
how naive we boys were about the war's
carnage and in most ways we men still are.

Dream Walker

Remember the dream walker, twelve years old
who wandered down the dormitory aisles,
lips trembling, hands brushing aside a cold
clump of stuck hair; our flashlight beams were dials
crazily glancing their numerals that might
implicitly be read on a pale clock
face where his features had been struck by light.
Night after night whatever dreams would stalk
him as he drifted past us lost their powers
to terrify as growing used to this
we slipped into our own oneiric towers
constructed from a personal abyss
of fears, desires but no compacted stones,
no thick blocks made from flesh, blood, or crushed bones.

Deliverance

Beneath a statue of the Sacred Heart
out in a courtyard we would fall in line.
One morning when we fooled around too much
Sister Angela swung her broom handle
at Dewayne Bailey and we went silent
watching as Bailey took one quick step toward
her, cutting the handle's arc, spreading his hands
along the shaft, and wrenching it from her
the way a martial artist would, then beat
her like a blanket making her habit
billow like a black flag falling when all
the pirate lanyards had been cut by swords.

Though in that moment fear broke loose and would
have run if it were water near our feet
across the hot asphalt, we were too shocked
to openly exult on that bright day.
Most of us knew Dewayne Bailey had more
rage than anyone we'd ever seen
before. And later when he put his head
down weeping at a desk in our classroom
waiting for Mother Superior's verdict
delivered by a black-robed messenger
from heaven or from hell most of us were
simply quiet like those forced to observe
some form of company punishment.
But then our eighth-grade Scottish nun bent down
and gently touched his head, her honey thick
brogue poured its healing balm over him.

Legacy

Grandfather stained the two-inch brown and light
tan squares where his chess pieces would one day
rest, ready for the game he'd never play
with me on his veranda on a hill
above the L.A. lights spread far below
like fields of diamonds glittering in the night.
He soaked the maple pieces in a tub,
bound them into a circle with iron clamps,
then glued the curved legs on, brushing the wood
with a shellac that's lasted all my life.

Ghost pieces now appear in dreams on squares
where my knights play havoc with pieces massed
around a rook beneath a shaking hand.
A mist enveloping the horse's head
makes my hand seem vague though I would grip
a silver bridal sketched on quivering air,
its lines erasing as I slowly turn
a black knight toward a radiant white queen.
Then wake up knowing grandfather has gone
forever "into a world of light" and I
will never learn from him—to build or choose
ghost pieces shuttling on that checkered board.

Dragon's Blood

I wondered what
these red rocks were.
I moved them like toys
across a desk kept
the way it was the day
grandfather put down his head,
his eyelids trembling
his heart flaring
then stopping forever.
Loose fingers brushed
a photo where he sat
astride a horse, cradling
instruments, something
like a sextant and a brass
tube in which the lines
of heat would magnify.
He'd close his eyes and fix
the spot where shafts would sink,
flecks of white pyrite glittering,
dust swirling up smoked
as the drills plunged.
The miners' faces darkened
white smudged their eyes
and ears, the slits were pink
and flickering tongues emerged
testing the air at dusk.
He may've thought
of other engineers
in other photos
their mustaches curled,
hair parted down the middle,
black suits and high white collars,
their dead, flat stares
that passed for dignity.
He saw them in khakis
bending above geological maps
lanterns sputtering.
They would trace each
gradient of rock, each tunnel

buttressed with trestles
as though they had crawled
on their bellies over
shale, powdered stone,
loose ore the Chinese
called "dragon's blood."
They crawled through the fetid air,
lungs full of dust.
When they found a new vein
they'd bring the veins
of the dragon in the mountain
to the surface and call
these red rocks drenched
with mercury, cinnabar.
I stacked the rocks
the way they were.

Grandmother Dreaming
(Her son John dead in Africa)

Grandmother sleeping thought her house
sat on a bluff above
the sea where fog and bells from buoys
wafted across a cove

below, terns crying in the night.
But all this ceased when John
withdrew his fingers from the keys
in a gray light one dawn.

His piano locked in a basement
could not now issue notes
lyrically pure on the salt air
where one gull feather floats

gathering to itself the last
light in grandmother's dream
until it darkens drifting down
where things rejected stream.

For a moment she thought her heart
had stopped when the struck cords
ended and no breaths came,
no gush of mumbled words.

Then eyes blink open and she hears
no notes shivering the air,
her son's return from Africa
impossible now for her.

He Died in Mexico

I learned today my brother had collapsed
in a shower as warm spray ran down a cheek.
A few nights after this I dreamed a light-
puffed towel slowly dropped from a shoulder,
bruised and pale beneath a febrile hand
which then refused to close before his head
struck tiles and rested at an angle there.
Consciousness swirled like water in a drain,
but he was spared a last indignity
watching some hostile neighbors pull his ruined
legs into a nylon body bag then zip
his nakedness into a final dark.
Even his body is now lost to us.

2.
They may have buried him in a mass grave
somewhere in Baja's Cabo San Jose.
We'll never visit a crude plot the blade
of a bulldozer ripped in the scorched earth.
By now they've capped his grave with cheap cement,
porous, already cracking with a few
wilting bouquets and with no view of blue-
green waves breaking on the Pacific shore
he loved so much. A few old women might
stand there silently weeping for men murdered
by sicarios. These may have been corpses
hung from steel girders of the bridge he strolled
past daily on his way to a taqueria
above the harbor's chartered fishing boats,
sails brightening in the sun above smooth decks.

3.
Oh let whatever may remain of him,
his soul or vague receding consciousness,
pass slowly toward the deep as though a sleek
hull could transport him there away from us.

Remember Jon Veinburg

1.
Remember how he crossed the infield
with adolescent friends when Tule fogs
obscured the playing fields. There would be Lance
Olson, the Derroian brothers and others
laughing and shoving each other. You could hear
them clear across the fields before at last
they would emerge from the gray mists, their breaths
pluming in front of them and Jon appeared
among them bundled up in his pea coat,
feisty, ducking some punches, jabbing the air.

2.
Imagine Jon in a white cubicle
reviewing files before his next client,
some hurt kid who would tentatively sit
in front of him like a trapped animal,
afraid, talking non-stop, eyes everywhere
or else defiant, sealed in a stone-like
silence till Jon elicited laughter
and finally a discussion of some lost
purpose abysmal conditions obscured.
Whatever anyone had done Jon claimed
he did something equivalent or worse.

3.
Remember Hanzlicek's on New Year's Eve.
Pete, Dixie, Fran, Mariana, Chuck, Dianne
laughing, drinking as Jon's and Phil Levine's
wit struck like flint on steel and lit the night
for us till tolling bells and the fireworks
blooming on a dark sky announced a new
year's arrival and we were all there.

4.
Recall how Jon would eat, drink, stay up late
with us, turn up the volume on a jazz
recording showing how this music might
exhibit parallels to the prosodies

we sometimes would defend or deconstruct
halfway through the night or until gray dawn appeared.
What now remains are Jon's inked syllables
in limited editions a reader might
thumb through on a hot day within the cool
shade cast by a Fig Garden elm and hear,
as if by chance, a voice risen from the page,
not wondering how Jon's body, slim as it
was, made such resonant lines when his heart
beat like the wings of hummingbirds and spilled
such iridescent colors on a page.
We will never hear again a voice like Jon's
emerging from the mists of Tule fogs
revealing fields on a cold winter day.

Pale Rider

For Peter Everwine

1.

Not long ago Peter lay down and slept
and did not wake again and though we live
four states away this news too quickly came
to us, not taking seasons to arrive.

A hundred years ago the leaves would turn
and telegraph lines ripped loose by gale force
winds rippling the dirt roads retarded news
then borne by a rider on a lathered horse.

When he galloped through rising summer heat
the clouds thrown up by hooves or a brief gust
could make him seem like an apocalyptic
horseman though he was only pale with dust.

2.

But words of friends expressing their distress
once sunk into something like a monk's cell
in his mind, pure, austere, or dropped like coins
to be laved by waters of a wishing well.

These wells were once contained by thick, stone walls,
not blood and bone where reddened lips restrain
syllables circulating in a throat
though these could rise in dreams echoing their pain.

When the last messenger appears above
your bed or in your car, his ripped shirt white,
streaked yellow or gray from roadside dust
blink back this herald of perpetual night.

And let each tear be a resplendent coin
charged with the hope there may be something more
for this poet who with his depth of feeling
may come to rest on a distant, well-lit shore.

Last Visit

For Roberto Bonazzi

When age or illness carves another self
from raw materials of a stressful life
one might anticipate features made pale
as limestone where time's blunted chisel moved
across the skin and bones. Where life endures
a little longer for this friend of ours.
And so we cross a parking lot and check
some building's numbers, but even before
we find his apartment we can see him
patiently waiting halfway in the shade,
half in the sun, which makes his wheelchair's arms
glow like gold plating on a chariot
a pharaoh would have plunged into the dark.
Roberto's battle now is more complex.
We push his chair along an empty walk
into a restaurant, try to converse.
His frail hands tremble on a water glass.
He silently eats lentils and pulled pork
like a convict bent to a final meal.
Oh Roberto let's avidly discuss
the world as we knew it a few years ago.
Let's resurrect those nights of wine and food,
assessments of paintings recently hung,
our latest poems, jazz, books, whatever moved
us through those nights before your words declined
and it was time to say good night dear friend.

Bars

Half opened blinds cast bars across my desk
as though to underline with light some things
I've misconstrued or put aside for weeks.
Could this now also symbolize how I
have locked myself from a dream's radiant field
where smiling relatives I've never met
beckon then slowly fade the way a snow
of light evaporates from film exposed
too soon though like an animal in a zoo
I'd hang there longing for what lies beyond?

Waiting

Not every maple leaf has reddened yet.
October temperatures are way too high.
There's no black ice disguised by roads made wet
with it and no bruised clouds cloaking the sky.

And yet it's time these things should reoccur.
We want to see the trees express bright plumes
before bare branches and thick trunks immure
themselves in glittering ice like winter blooms.

We know the seasons had a rhythm we
once thought we felt like pulses in our wrists.
Today we've only heard wind rake a tree
drying in a yard scoured by dusty mists.

Fall

Driving over roads in upper Michigan
we have observed how leaves massed overhead,
have changed their colors, readying themselves
for their slow spiral down our instincts dread.

Trees bear their final shades of green, mauve, orange,
red, yellows now so vivid leaves may merge
with light and flicker like wind-trebled tongues
above us as we pass this brilliant dirge.

Sky Flowers

It's sunset when Lake Michigan becomes
a sheet of silver where the melting sun
splashes color so lovely it almost numbs
the eyes observing this as night comes on.

Darkness invariably slides across
the waters like eyelids shutting down,
not many pin-pricked stars, no southern cross,
a few illuminations by the moon.

But I remember how the northern lights
briefly obstruct the darkness when a plume
of green appears and suddenly ignites
a plot of the sky with a shivering bloom.

Fox Light

Dusk on the country road
above our house, a fox
observes me as I trudge
uphill gripping my staff.
He pauses for twenty
seconds or so, his tail
roped side to side before
he sprints into the brush.
Dim light grays his fur, which should
be red or brown, but colors
mute, even vibrant green shades
before a red sun drops in the west.

Later my wife will say
a fox allowing this
encounter means you're blessed.
You might now share the eyes
of the red fox as though
you peer into a night scope
bolted to a rifle barrel.
Then be a fox stalking geese
in a neighbor's yard, teeth
ripping through a long neck,
devouring the head only,
leaving a clump of white
feathers in our front yard.

Disguise

The sun has left brown patches where we'll stride
carefully because a coral snake emerged
from a leaf-pile; a neighbor saw it slide
through mottled light where leaves and colors merged.

The red bands touching yellows made it clear
this could not be a king snake on the dirt,
then grass, then pebbles gliding way too near.
At first a struck bare leg will seldom hurt.

But soon the neurotoxins will begin
sensual derangements, hedges buzzing pale
pink, a vein seeming to protrude from skin
on the side of a leg like a bent nail.

There could be respiratory obstruction
or none if one would quickly rip the fangs
loose, hurling gorgeous loops against the sun,
expecting still, cold sweats and heart-deep pangs.

Dispassion

Observing the neighbor's rural fenced-in lot
where chickens, ducks, turkeys and two lab dogs
cavort I watch the rescued paint horse trot
to a distant corner where mud-slathered hogs
grunting above their slops nudge the thick boards
penning them in, but the stoical horse,
immersed in thought, bends to the tiny swords
of grass dawn light edges against the coarse
textures of his tongue gliding over them.
He would escape the drama and the din,
the storm of feathers making a white hem
quiver along fetlocks in a cold wind.

My Auto De Fe

The air is smoke.
Highways are metal. They glitter
with a carapace of cars and trucks,
lines of beetles inching forward.
Though stubble is gold, the earth
darkens where someone flicked
a cigarette from a car window.
And yet somehow this flame-licked
land of ours endures another season
though it needs rain, rain and more rain.

Drive this landscape, sealed
behind safety glass
and parched, eviscerate trees
might seem as unreal
as unbelievers stacked for burning.

Ruined Towns

We drive through some out of curiosity
on our way west or south leaving the main
highways which have bypassed once thriving towns.
Some stucco buildings lining the town squares
have storefront windows plywood sheets have sealed
like blinded eyes with no reflections, gray
as though glaucoma or fists put them out.
Think of men toiling in the summer heat
or winter frost erecting these structures
which last beyond hopes for prosperity.
Even the walls of some rocked houses fall
because someone diluted the mortar
with substances now crumbling white as salt.
Some stones ajar now seem like carious teeth
in a jaw broken by a club or fist.
We drive by trying to forget these scenes.

John Brewer Loves Hardwoods

only hardwoods like white
oak, red oak, long leaf pine.
He describes their properties
with the fervor of a man
whose hands would shape for us
a woman's curves, her hips
fluid as she moves toward him
in a dream murmuring his name.
With absolute precision
he'll settle white oak planks
over spaces we'll soon tread.
Will he consider how
this wood was nourished once
by deeply plunging roots
into the fecund earth?

My Birthday Staff
For Scott

He broke a branch from a squat mesquite tree,
weighed the gnarled length in his right hand, stripped leaves,
smoothed it with pieces of sand paper, brushed
on a coat of varnish or linseed oil
or something else. When the oil dried, the staff
glowed yellow gold and Scott then burned the top
circle with my initials, handing it
to me on my birthday, knowing I'd use
it when I trudged uphill behind our house
where deer, wild pigs and the elusive fox
keep watch in leafy shadows, eyes like dots
of light in a green darkness where they lurk.
The little terrier who barks too much
and tries to nip ankles and heels must now
maintain respectful distances or just
one time feel a hard knot against his jaw.

I love the heft of it and twirling it
overhead make it swish like raptor wings
diving at high speed onto a bare neck.
I now remember how a friend and I
would bang oak staffs together out in the yard
after a movie in which Friar Tuck
spilled from a calf skin saddle onto dirt
an evil sheriff's man down, Tuck's staff
singing through dappled light beneath huge trunks.

Observing Her

Unashamed I compare my love to a swan
floating perpetually across
memory's green or blue expanse.
The thin white wakes crisscross
melting like sutures, leaving no scars,
pocked briefly with a sprinkling of stars.

Long strides consuming distances never
cut a foaming arc
across the air or water like webbed
feet pulsing through the dark.
But I have seen her glide through space
with her own equivalent grace.

At times like this she seems as lovely
as the white swan paddling beyond
my reach across the gunwale of a boat
tipping toward a pond
when I bend to damp feathers on the deck
or salt-soaked tresses on her neck.

Without white plumage she'll float down trails,
Silver tipping her fingers and toes.
Moonlight glazes the rims of her glasses,
circling ice-blue floes,
lightly dusting her shoulders bare
and arms and massed blonde hair.

Balance

Adjusting the angle of a painting's edge,
dusting book shelves as she glides
from room to room and leaves a sense
of order there even as she slides
on a loosened rug and rights
herself in a dazzle of lights.

Let her imagine the whir and pulse
felt when a loose gear spun
in a watch's locked case flashing on her wrist.
Her perfect balance would shun
disordered movement and an internal pendulum
instantly restore her equilibrium.

Legs

Coach said, "Davis, your legs are like tree trunks."
Rooting myself I'd block a surging end
and I remember driving blocking sleds
further than anyone on my high school
football team, foam rubber above my ears
sweat damp, my jersey soaked in the hot sun
of early September, remember how
we longed for water as we galloped up
poison oak hill in full armor, our cleats
pocking the grass of the hillside beneath
a scattering of oaks, a few fir trunks.
But now in age legs often buckle, sway
when strenuous exertion taxes them.
Oh lord my legs get weaker day by day.

My wife's long tapering legs, perfectly curved,
eat distances of ground whenever we
try walking together on a park trail
or heading down some harbor esplanade.
We'll pause watching some turquoise waves fleck white
in a strong breeze, then walk again and she'd
be gone in a minute till circling back
after she lapped me, we'd continue our talk
then she'd be gone again, mercurial legs
transporting her so swiftly I almost
hear a thresh thresh of the invisible wings
above her ankles, not thinking this is
wind caught among the leaves of stricken elms.

New Wound

An old man tripped and fell on a stone ledge.
His blood dripped into a leaf shape so red
and brilliant on the jagged brown there might
have been a painter who would slice an arm
to streak a canvas with a hue like this—
gorgeous on brown rocks veined with silica
emerging from the pool as sunlight shone
brightly there when wind shifted plush branches.

Winter

I
Observe men vitrified on cups
stacked neatly in their blue
ranks near a sink, none soft, alive,
each baked in a blue tattoo

depicting scholars who must bend
above manuscripts year
after year till their neck bones fuse,
each spine like a bent spear.

II
Some yellow dragon blossoms glow
in an oblong of light
outside the window near my desk
though early winter blight

has blanched so many leaves and made
some other petals droop.
How long can any blossom drink
pale light and never stoop?

Diagnosis

Brass keys mingling with other keys might rest
forever in a kitchen cabinet.
But in our rooms of flesh and blood we may
have stored disjecta of our memories,
tattered and blurred, slipped into consciousness
with no obvious movement of the will,
no effort to expunge the spots a robe
of conscience bears like ink spilled or bloodshed,
deeply worked into the imagined fibers
skilled craftsmen might have weaved into new bolts
of wool, soft on the skin as a silk shirt.
The doctor did not say, "Your brain can be
its own place ruled by nothing anyone
else says or does." There may be tiny rooms
membranes would have sealed like the doors we locked.
But if these portals somehow could be pierced
the graven world might blossom then against
the leaves of memory or a struck brain
and one might haul into the light again
moments throbbing like tarpons on lodged hooks.

Apocalypse

Let consciousness flicker like a lamp's bulb
before the bulb blows out in a cold place
dimming a broken chain and coarse rock walls.
But in this dream a man might glimpse a pale
embrasure washed with light, the sun and moon
still transiting invisible arcs far, far
above as fitfully he turns through dreams
repeated nightly for a month or so.
Too many trivial pursuits along
with the minutiae of his daily life
blanched memory so often now he moves
through bright days with a vague uneasiness.

Revelation

If existence could be like tattered robes,
moth holes, soup stains fading the scarlet dye,
a man might touch his neck as though the harsh
cloth rubbed red the skin there, loose folds awry.

A tiny gold chain broken near the throat
might've held a cloak in place, not let a sword
arm tangle in swirled cloth when others burst
upon a littered field their shed blood scored.

Perhaps some men must wear something like this
into eternity, their stenciled crimes
soaking through cloth would tattoo their skins blue,
if they have skin, eyes glittering like new dimes.

Revelation 2

My partially closed shades let bars of light
run slant-wise down a yellow page. My pen
marks it with webs of ink as copious
as the excretions threatened squids employ
to cloak them from their shark-like predators.
A person lingering in my streaked mirror
is only partially realized there,
knowledge of what he is obscured by dark
cursives spread from my hand. But if somehow
I gripped one bar of light and trained
it like a torch on whatever coats the glass
like oil spilled on a pond, burning it off
would images of a whole self shimmer there?

But I Have Bad Dreams

Fear of the virus makes us stay
inside or pull on masks and gloves
keeping safe distances at stores.
We smile and wave at those we love.

But dream our neighbors rove like wolves
across dew frosted lawns and leave
misshapen prints of paws or hooves
among the sparkling, moon tipped blades.

Tonight I may witness again
evidence of disease encased
so firmly in a dream's gouged clefts
it won't be easily erased.

After the Storm

Effects of light may go
unnoticed for awhile
like a tracery of snow
on broad leaves a light oil
or something else has smeared
reflecting for a moment
bright planes a hot wind tiered.
Aeolus might have sent
this kind of semaphore
by way of leaves or clouds
to let the caught winds roar
from caves dropping loose shrouds
of matter anywhere
on anything: roof tiles,
thatch, a stained shirt and bare
branches, no leaf shaped aisles
leading our eyes to the sun,
most rippling leaves spun down.

Winds

The trees were busy all night long.
Leaves loosened their wind songs.
Our dreams articulated notes
uncoiled from their harsh tongues.

Rooted and listening near us year
by year what have the great
oaks learned and what leaved syllables
did wild winds lacerate?

Falling

When a rectangle of pure light
quivered on the oak floor
of our long hall then disappeared
like a tide covered shore

rippling beyond me in a dream
in which I blinked and turned
back to a book splayed beside me
like something I had spurned

because black print had not sunk deep
in pages radiant
as snow to stabilize the torn
papers driven aslant

and darkly crinkling in a wind
nightmare secretions once
stained with sepias of fear
anxiety, malice

but this is how these things come down
falling and falling where
nothing exists except piled up stones,
gray, pitted and too bare.

The Day After

On resurrection's first day don't make me
search upturned grave sites, ashes blown
on my skin, hair and lips, gray monuments
tumbled like mountain stones in an earthquake.
What happened to the angel's trumpet, brass
notes ringing through the air, if there is air?
Will forms, eternal patterns, bring back bones
dressing them with flesh, a loaded brush
or something like one wiped across skin, hair
make vivid colors re-emerge? I'll look
my love for the spun gold of your blonde head.

Indoor Plants

The plant upon my desk has broad, green leaves
two inches wide, six inches long which do
not droop the way unwatered plants would droop
over the edges of an orange pot.
It's based on two stacked saucers blue and gold
with what could be Arabic calligraphies
or a representation of writhing roots
pulled up and lacquered on the porcelain.
A plant like this is not supposed to thrive
on air the way aerial orchids do,
suspended in mid-flight and loosely bound
by tendrils to a trunk: they tremble up
above green filtered light on jungle floors.
It seems no one has poured even a half
full glass onto the gray crust of its dirt.
Yet it survives month after month in front
of me as I bend to my written tasks.
Once in a dream my lavender shirts pulsed
with light and rose like orchids blossoming,
pierced feet protruding tethered by silk threads,
shirts fed only by aerial currents
where flocks of gorgeous parrots mock and swirl.

Entreaty

Temper my will into something like steel
bars forged in furnaces before they're pulled
into the air to cool and harden, then may I
sit at a desk piled high with manuscripts
letting a black rain fall from my right hand
to clutter the pages of a legal pad
dream-blurring eyes would ripple into fields
of mustard briefly ruled by straight, green lines.
My pen's black specklings could be like stunned bees
spilled from hives crushed beneath a tractor's treads.
I'd move in my mind almost anywhere
despite my body's new, disrupted sense
of balance when I rise from rickety chairs.
But let a cultivated purpose gleam
like an edged blade introduced to the light.
And let my body be the scabbard.

Entreaty 2

What makes a cactus blossom writhe
in sunlight with no wind?
Bend to a yellow cup and look
within where you will find

small beetles who will eat and spread
to almost every inch
of a soft, gold interior.
This view should make you flinch

from desecrations such as this:
something once beautiful
whose transitory luster turns
too swiftly brown and dulls.

Before voracious insects blight
their petaled glory, let
blossoms maintain a brief tenure
against a mortal debt.

Entreaty 3

Allow my joints to bend more fluidly
even when blankets weigh on aching legs
and throbbing knees whose bending may ease pain
sometimes late in the night, sometimes at dawn.
Too often this will block a slow drift back
to sleeping and dreaming pleasantly
before my time-piece pulses on my wrist
and I must rise to face a summer day
then through a window glance into the yard
where rows of flowers line jagged, stone paths.
The brilliant colors draw some butterflies.
Their wings beat rapidly above a swirl
of corollas where they would sink and cease
for a moment their efforts to transcribe
their colors on the air or anywhere
they choose if somehow this were possible.
Oh let these heavy bones now sprout a cape
of feathers brightening on the air and lift
me from the grim necessities of age.

Eating Flowers

1.
Deer eat our flowers almost every night.
The yellow Esperanza blooms are gone.
Blue Morning Glory buds have disappeared,
their shortened stems quiver in a cold wind,
a cruel precursor of our winter nights.
Because they sense the winter's liquid ice
will coat and harden on grass blades and stems
and falling leaves are brown, deer fatten now
on cherished plants we thought they'd leave alone.

I dream of shot gun slugs, poisons, bear trap's
huge, spring driven teeth and a mean dog
lunging, uncoiling a long chain held taut
as guitar strings too tightly strung with shrill
notes plucked from steel links by his muscled chest
and the Aeolian energies the wind
unleashes as deer sprint into the dark.

2.
If Van Gogh ate from a palette
why not put petals in your mouth
and stain your lips gold, purple, red
reappearing in the kitchen at dusk,
startling your wife as though she might
imagine a white skull wearing through skin
not trimmed in a black mask the way
it would've been on the day of the dead.

And in this crazy mood admire
yourself in a hallway mirror,
hoping the colored rivulets
coursed down the corner of your mouth,
marking the creases sorrow carved.
But if there are only two faint
fluorescent paths, yellow, light green,
enough of these lapping your chin,
spilling onto your chest, your new

shirt stained forever, something
within may sprout iridescent buds
in your blurred eyes or in your dreams.

Body Armor

The metal is light, lighter than feathers
and the gold river cools your hand
the imaginary pure hand and the aching muscles.
Someone holds it up to the light
and the white felt liner rubs against your cheek.

But the thick body weighted with hamstring
with the blood of a tackle crusting your forearm
with all your little murders is shy, dazzled, childlike.
Someone says take it. Someone says it's yours
and if you close your eyes your torso will gleam.

When you open them there's the locker room
and the burning salts. The plastic shoulder pads
and the foam rubber damp with sweat.
Your taped hands buckle and tighten.
Oil of wintergreen burns and cools a river of bruises.

To walk again in the waterfalls of iron
and harm no one. The pure right hand undarkened
by the hot sail billowing through the blood
the firm new flesh unharnessed
and the breathing walls of light raising you up.

www.ingramcontent.com/pod-product-compliance
Lightning Source LLC
Chambersburg PA
CBHW021403090426
42742CB00009B/986